LANGUAGE, CULTURE AND
CARIBBEAN IDENTITY

LANGUAGE, CULTURE AND
CARIBBEAN IDENTITY

Edited by

Jeannette Allsopp and John R. Rickford

Canoe Press

Jamaica • Barbados • Trinidad and Tobago

Centre for Caribbean Lexicography
University of the West Indies

Canoe Press
7A Gibraltar Hall Road, Mona
Kingston 7, Jamaica
www.uwipress.com

Centre for Caribbean Lexicography
University of the West Indies
Cave Hill, Barbados

© 2012 by Jeannette Allsopp and John R. Rickford

All rights reserved. Published 2012

A catalogue record of this book is available from the National Library of Jamaica.

ISBN: 978-976-8125-92-7

Cover illustration: Brianna McCarthy, *Maker Self*.
By courtesy of the artist.
Cover design by Richard Mark Rawlins.
Printed in the United States of America.

CONTENTS

Introduction   1
Jeannette Allsopp and John R. Rickford

PART 1 CARIBBEAN ENGLISH

1. Whither English in the Caribbean?   9
Pauline Christie

PART 2 CREOLE LINGUISTICS IN THE CARIBBEAN

2. The Creole Concept in Culture Studies: A Revaluation   19
Mervyn C. Alleyne

3. Reduplication and Language Change in Guyana   29
Alim Hosein

4. The Future Markers in Urban and Rural Guyanese Creole   43
Walter F. Edwards

5. The Social *and* the Linguistic in Sociolinguistic Variation: *Mii en noo* (Me ain' know)   51
John R. Rickford

PART 3 CARIBBEAN LEXICOGRAPHY

6. The *DCEU* Sets Sail from Bridgetown on Friday, 26 April 1996 . . .   63
John Simpson

7. "Coolie Types": On the Use of Photo Elicitation in Collecting and Verifying Indic Lexicon in Trinidad and Tobago   69
Lise Winer

8. Caribbean Lexicography: A Chronicle of the Linguistic and Cultural Identity of One People   81
Jeannette Allsopp

CONTENTS

PART 4 CARIBBEAN FOLKLORE AND RELIGION

9 In Support of Afrogenesis: A Study of St Lucian French Creole Proverbs — 93
   Hazel Simmons-McDonald

10 Mingi Mamma: Continuities and Metamorphoses in a Colonial Context — 107
    Ian E. Robertson

11 Comfa — 115
    Kean Gibson

PART 5 CARIBBEAN LITERATURE, MUSIC AND DANCE

12 Narrative as Autobiography of the Folk — 123
    Velma Pollard

13 The Effective Use of Literary Devices in the Calypso — 129
    Claudith Thompson

14 Constructing French Creole Identity through Language, Music and Dance: A Focus on Guadeloupe and Martinique — 139
    Hélène Zamor

PART 6 LANGUAGE ISSUES IN CARIBBEAN SCHOOLS

15 A Folkloric Approach to Literacy: Addressing Semantic Confusion in a Bilingual Community — 151
    Martha F. Isaac

16 Boys Will Be Boys: Gender and Bilingual Education in a Creole Language Situation — 161
    Karen Carpenter and Hubert Devonish

Contributors — 177

INTRODUCTION

Jeannette Allsopp and
John R. Rickford

When the idea first came to Jeannette to put together a publication to commemorate the life and work of the late Richard Allsopp, Caribbean linguist extraordinaire, pioneering lexicographer and cultural researcher, she knew immediately whom she would ask to participate in this venture as co-editor. Professor John R. Rickford was both a student and a lifelong friend of Richard's and also a colleague as well as a friend of Jeannette's, the two of them having both lectured at the University of Guyana in the 1970s. Their close friend and colleague Professor Ian Robertson (recently retired from the University of the West Indies) had already co-edited a special edition of *Kyk-over-Al* in Richard's honour in 1998, and so they also owe him a debt of gratitude, which they must acknowledge, especially as he is also a contributor to this publication.

There is perhaps no more fitting tribute to a scholar than to be celebrated by his peers, especially through a festschrift that includes their work. This publication certainly reflects that through its contents. The authors who contributed to this volume all fall into the category of Richard's former students, friends or colleagues and are each, in their own fields, outstanding contributors to Caribbean linguistics in general and a few to Caribbean lexicography in particular.

The volume consists of sixteen chapters (including those of the two editors) and this introduction, as well as biographical notes on each author. The articles are varied in their scope and cover the wide-ranging interests of Richard in language in general, literacy, linguistics, lexicography and culture.

The articles fall into six broad categories: Caribbean English, Creole linguistics in the Caribbean, Caribbean lexicography, Caribbean folklore and religion, Caribbean literature, music and dance, and language issues in Caribbean schools.

Caribbean English

In the sole contribution in this category, **Pauline Christie** explores Richard Allsopp's major lifelong interest, the question of the current status and function of English in the Caribbean. She considers the factors that influence its development and the acceptability of local varieties as well as attitudes towards those varieties and maps out a vision of the future of English in the Caribbean.

Creole Linguistics in the Caribbean

Mervyn C. Alleyne provides a critical discussion of the term *Creole* in relation to Caribbean language, people and culture. Among other things, he surveys its different referents and usage in Trinidad, Martinique, Puerto Rico and Jamaica and compares it with terms such as *classical, folk* and *wild*, which represent control through language imposition by the powerful. He ends by noting the need to promote positive evaluations of the black populations in the Caribbean before addressing Creole identities, a legacy of the colonial past. **Alim Hosein** looks at reduplication and language change in Guyana. He reports that a wide range of respondents from different areas claim to recognize and use examples of reduplication. He then analyses reduplications collected from everyday life and the media, revealing the wide range of linguistic functions they serve. The ubiquity and vitality of reduplication, he argues, indicate that the Creole vernacular is alive and well and that decreolization is not occurring. **Walter Edwards** discusses and analyses in detail the future markers *go* and *gun* (sometimes represented as *gon*) in Guyanese urban and rural Creole, providing insights into their use and considering the question of whether they should be related to an irrealis category of modals as well as looking at the sociolinguistic implications of their use. He discusses the strange disappearance of *sa* as a future marker in modern Guyanese and concludes that rural Guyanese *go* and rural/urban Guyanese *gun* derive from different sources. **John R. Rickford** emphasizes that sociolinguistic variation in language is jointly influenced by (and influences) the social *and* the linguistic. Using quantitative data, he examines morphological and phonological variation in Guyanese personal pronouns, showing that although the variants convey important information about the speakers' social class, style, urban/rural background and gender, they are also influenced by internal linguistic constraints, some of them first demonstrated by Richard Allsopp in 1958, before the work of William Labov, Derek Bickerton, and other variationists.

Caribbean Lexicography

John Simpson, a lexicographer of British English and the editor of the third volume of the *Oxford English Dictionary*, looks at the launch of the *Dictionary of Caribbean English Usage* and the implications of that publication for Caribbean lexicography and its position within general English lexicography, which he says Caribbean lexicography will help to expand. He also looks at the future of Caribbean lexicography and at the fact that Richard Allsopp's pioneering work in Caribbean lexicography has given rise to a full Centre for Caribbean Lexicography, which not only carries on the actual work of dictionary production but has also produced – and is producing – a new crop of graduate students who will ensure its continuation. **Lise Winer**'s chapter describes and analyses the technique of using historical photographs to elicit and specify lexical items, with specific reference to the domain of traditional Indian jewellery in Trinidad. It also looks at ethical, cultural and epistemological concerns within the particular context, and it seeks to encourage other researchers, particularly lexicographers and ethnographers working in the Caribbean, to make greater use of archival photo elicitations in their research. **Jeannette Allsopp** demonstrates the linguistic and cultural similarities in various aspects of Caribbean life and discusses the concept of identity against a theoretical background, showing that there is one Caribbean identity. Allsopp also uses a number of examples from Caribbean dictionaries across Caribbean languages to illustrate the role of Caribbean lexicography as a linguistic and cultural record of the entire range of Caribbean life and culture.

Caribbean Folklore and Religion

Hazel Simmons-McDonald extends and supports Richard Allsopp's thesis on the Afrogenesis of Caribbean Creoles and Caribbean Creole proverbs in her work on the Afrogenesis of French Creole proverbs by showing African correlates to a number of the proverbs in a number of life situations and provides invaluable information on the interrelationship between anglophone and francophone Creole proverbs.

Ian Robertson focuses on a Guyanese folkloric character, Mamma Mingi, the Berbice Dutch equivalent for Water Mamma, a commonly known folkloric character throughout the Caribbean. (Compare Mama Glo in the French Creole territories.) He highlights the West African continuities of language and culture to be found in Berbice Dutch by linking the historical, linguistic and cultural influences to be found in that language variety. He also links the character with spiritual practices of the slaves in Berbice and cross-references it with an Amerindian spirit, Kanaima, showing certain similarities with the West African spirit.

Kean Gibson examines Comfa, the adaptation of the African religion of Comfa to the Guyanese context, in that rather than worshipping direct ancestors, the practitioners worship spirits of the different ethnicities who at one time or another populated Guyana. Gibson goes on to show that despite the fact that practitioners worship spirits of different ethnicities, there is a communal spirit within the religion which is in no way related to the divided society in which the religion is created and practised.

Caribbean Literature, Music and Dance

Velma Pollard considers narrative and autobiography and concludes that narrative is essentially the autobiography of cities and villages and the people who inhabit them. She finds that narrative is autobiography, not biography, because the villages and people tell their own stories, describe their own lives and expose their own attitudes, though these may be modified by the imagination of the author. She illustrates this with two short stories by Olive Senior, examined from the perspective of such concepts as race, religion and class.

Claudith Thompson looks at the use of double entendre, humour, sarcasm/irony and literary devices in Caribbean calypso, with special reference to major calypsonians in Guyana, Barbados and Trinidad. She defines calypso, outlines its characteristics and then discusses the use of a variety of literary devices, such as personification, illustrating the fact that such devices serve to enrich the genre of calypso and to provide penetrating social commentary as well as entertainment for the public.

Hélène Zamor examines the construction of a French Creole identity through French Caribbean language, music and dance and considers creolization, which brought about the French Creole language, as itself an identity marker. She compares this with the French colonial policy of departmentalization, which created a schizophrenic sense of identity in French Caribbean people, who are still considered French by the metropolitan government. Zamor shows how the development of creolized forms of French Caribbean music and dance help to foster a French Caribbean identity.

Language Issues in Caribbean Schools

Martha Isaac discusses the problem of semantic confusion experienced by young students in a bilingual community, who speak either French or English-based Creole, or both, alongside the official language. The chapter proposes a pedagogy that acknowledges the sociocultural contexts of education in a bilingual community as well as the lexical components which are inherently problematic in that context. This is an area with which Richard Allsopp was quite preoccupied and therefore adds to the dimension of the publication in general

Karen Carpenter and Hubert Devonish discuss an unexpected outcome of a body of research surrounding the Bilingual Education Project in Jamaica, a research project which involved the use, for all educational functions, of English, the traditional language of education, and Jamaican (Jamaican Creole) over the first four years of primary education in a Jamaican primary school. Carpenter and Devonish provide the slant of gender in their study of the project supported by quantitative research data.

In general, the volume is a wide-ranging one which we hope will be of great interest and use to a number of scholars in Caribbean linguistics, language education, culture and lexicography even as it commemorates the scope of Richard Allsopp's academic and cultural interests and preoccupations throughout the long years of his distinguished career as a Caribbean linguist and lexicographer.

The volume is also particularly significant in that it reflects the continuation of Allsopp's life work through the Centre for Caribbean Lexicography at the

University of the West Indies at Cave Hill, now directed by Jeannette Allsopp, one of the two editors of this work. It is the second collaborative publication between the Centre for Caribbean Lexicography and the University of the West Indies Press, the first one being the *New Register of Caribbean English Usage* (2010), which was Richard Allsopp's last work, published posthumously. Having the current work appear in 2012 is a great honour for the centre, as 2012 marks the fortieth year of institutionalized Caribbean lexicography at the University of the West Indies at Cave Hill campus, the original Caribbean lexicography project having begun in 1972. It is also a significant occasion for the Society for Caribbean Linguistics, which is hosting in 2012 its nineteenth biennial conference in the Bahamas. Co-editor Jeannette Allsopp is the current president of the Society for Caribbean Linguistics. Richard Allsopp was a past president and vice president as well as a life member, and the appearance of this book on this occasion represents a double tribute to him.

It is therefore the hope of the editors that this historically and academically significant publication will fulfil the objectives that motivated its production and stand as a lasting tribute to Richard Allsopp, pioneering Caribbean Creole linguist and lexicographer.

Part 1

Caribbean English

Chapter 1

WHITHER ENGLISH IN THE CARIBBEAN?

Pauline Christie

Over the past three decades or so, several harsh comments about the current state of English in Jamaica have appeared in the local press at regular intervals. For example, two letters, one submitted to the *Gleaner* in 1994 and one to the *Jamaica Observer* in 2004, appeared under the headings "The Assassination of English" and "Slaughtering the English Language".[1] These phrases had been used by the correspondents in question. An additional point worth noting is that the two letters were written ten years apart, evidence of the persistence of the concern they expressed.

The arguments usually provided to support the view that standards in English have been declining include reference to poor examination results in the Caribbean Secondary Education Certificate examinations and the fact that some university entrants are now required to sit a proficiency test in English, which has a high failure rate. This state of affairs is frequently contrasted with the high standard of English allegedly achieved by products of the elementary schools of the past.

This reaction is illustrated in a *Gleaner* editorial, which read in part, "There is no doubt that in earlier years, our students in general were much more competent in the use and application of the language. Few people then attained the old Sixth Standard in Elementary School without acquiring a good working knowledge of English. Today, there are many reports of university graduates with poor skills in the language" (5 April 1994).

Irvine (2004, 66) has expressed the view that phonological variation is likely to be the important determinant of good English in Jamaica, particularly for educated speakers. Justifying this conclusion is the fact that those persons who claim that English is under threat usually single out aspects of pronunciation for special criticism. For example, one newspaper columnist, a former teacher, complained as follows: "These days, as you listen to voices on and off the electronic media, it is disgusting to hear so many of the people who should know better, the people who are representative of the best in Jamaica and who define us beyond our shores – people from Parliament, pulpit, private sector, professions, university, police, media – fail to properly pronounce even commonplace words" (Chester Burgess, *Gleaner*, 11 September 1999).

The usual examples of the so-called improper pronunciation include features which are clearly influenced by the Creole vernacular, for example,

(a) *h* dropping, as in /istri/ instead of /histri/ for *history*;[2]
(b) substitution of the alveolar nasal /n/ for its velar counterpart /ng/ in *ing*;
(c) palatalization of /k/ and /g/ before /a/, as in /kyap/ for *cap* and /gyap/ for *gap*;
(d) metathesis, as in /aks/ for *ask*, and the reversal of the vowels in the first syllable of the word *violence*;
(e) alveolar stops /t/ and /d/ for interdental fricatives in words spelled with *th*, for example, *thing* and *this*, respectively;
(f) reduction of word-final consonant clusters as in, for example, /mos/ for *must* and /fain/ for *find*.

There is also evidence of hypercorrection. Thus one often finds, for example,

(a) initial /h/ added to words pronounced with an initial vowel in generally accepted Standard English, for example, *is* pronounced /hiz/;
(b) emphasis on the second consonant in word-final consonant clusters.

All these departures from the norm have traditionally been stigmatized, but they have become increasingly common in the formal usage of even highly educated persons.

Stress placement is another area where departures from the traditional norm are spreading. In the formal speech of many highly educated persons, one hears stress on the second syllables of, for example, *reGISter, chaRACter, comMERCE, mainTENance, ManCHESter,* instead of the first, and on the final syllables of *conriBUTE* and *distriBUTE* instead of the second.

There is a strong tendency on the part of older persons to blame the so-called decline of English on the contrast between current teaching methods and those which were used in the past. For example, they point out that strong emphasis was placed in earlier days on teaching explicitly stated rules of grammar and spelling, which learners were expected to memorize. In fact, several writers in Jamaican newspapers refer nostalgically to having closely studied Nesfield's *English Grammar*, a popular school textbook in "the good old days". Some older persons also express regret that Latin is no longer taught in school, as they claim that learning Latin taught them English grammar. Teachers of an earlier day are also held up as good models of English, allegedly more proficient in it than their successors.

Introduced as the official language under colonialism, English has been the official medium of education in Jamaica for approximately two centuries. It is also the traditional language of administration and churches. Its high status was reinforced by the roles traditionally assigned to it and by contrast with the relatively low status of the Creole vernacular, which is still viewed by most Jamaicans as bad English. Furthermore, whereas English has traditionally been associated with both written and spoken language, Creole, with no generally recognized writing system, has been largely confined to oral use.

The past few decades have witnessed the loosening of ties with Britain following Jamaica's political independence in 1962 and growing consciousness of a Jamaican identity, alongside other social changes, including greater social mobility. In addition, there has been greater acceptance of Creole in roles which formerly required English exclusively. For example, Creole has almost superseded English in the theatre, and it is now often used in advertisements on radio and television and in the newspapers.

The British concept of Standard English that was instilled into Jamaican schoolchildren over many years and that was constantly reinforced by the traditional teaching methods was of a uniform ideal, associated with the elite. Before independence, teachers in the relatively few secondary schools and teachers' colleges were often imported from Britain or had been taught by such persons. The textbooks and other printed material which promoted the projected ideal were also from that source. Allowance was made as regards some pronunciations, largely because even the British-born teachers tended not to be users of Received Pronunciation.

Another noticeable feature of Jamaican English is the growing influence of American English. Such influence is not at all new. However, it has spread more widely in recent decades as a result of increasing personal and business contacts and tourism and also through electronic media – radio, television and, most recently, the Internet. Some Jamaican radio personalities deliberately adopt an American accent, but these are fewer than in the past.

If questioned, many Jamaicans would still express a preference for traditional British usage over its American counterpart (see, for example, Sand 2011, 169). However, they are often unaware of specific differences between American usage and the traditional British standard; therefore much of the borrowing is unconscious. At the same time, an increasing number of persons now have access to the Internet, where the checks on spelling and grammar are based on American English. The fact that the *Gleaner* sponsors annual participation by some secondary schools in the popular Scripps National Spelling Bee in Washington, DC, is further evidence that British English no longer has a monopoly.

The label "Standard Jamaican English" (SJE), which is often used nowadays, is apparently intended to represent the formal usage expected from educated Jamaicans. However, it is not clear if those who use it are referring to an idealization or a reality or if, in either case, it includes both spoken and written language. It might even sometimes simply reflect the search for a national identity and the related attitude to external norms as much as, or even perhaps instead of, being based on specific linguistic characteristics.

Despite this vagueness, the concept of a local standard is not at all far-fetched. Fifty years ago, De Camp (1961, 83) had commented, "Whether Jamaicans realize it or not, whether they want it or not, a Jamaican Standard English is gradually and inevitably emerging, equivalent in status to, but different in form from, the standards of England and the United States."

In many countries throughout the world today, the idea that Standard English must be synonymous with British Standard English is no longer accepted. English is now seen as a heterogeneous language with different norms in different countries. For some time now, American Standard English has been widely recognized and accepted. More recently, Australian English, Canadian English and Indian English have also been identified beyond their national boundaries. So, too, have a host of others that have been termed *New Englishes*, used in parts of Asia and Africa in particular. The new norms are based on actual usage in the countries rather than on a vague foreign ideal. This was an inevitable development, as the language of a people inevitably reflects its sense of its own identity and its culture. Even British Standard English is constantly changing. For example, since the end of World War II, it, too, has been more and more influenced by American English.

The problem lies in knowing where to draw the line between what should be considered part of SJE and what should still be attributed to error. The question of acceptability is therefore of the utmost importance. Pronunciation and orthographical differences between the traditional standard and actual usage are naturally the most conspicuous, hence these account for most of the examples provided by those who complain about the alleged decline of English in Jamaica. However, because there is often a close link between lexicon and culture, many differences at this level are readily accepted, hence the relevance of focus on dictionaries.

Another question which has to be asked concerning SJE is "Who sets the new standards?" Formal usage of well-educated Jamaicans that departs from the traditional norm is not automatically considered acceptable, as the comments presented earlier indicate. At one extreme are persons who firmly insist on the old standards without exception, even including some rules that are now considered outdated in Britain or the United States. One can easily distinguish between such purists, who wince at every occurrence of a split infinitive or a sentence-final preposition, and persons at the other extreme who appear not to be bothered by such matters. Besides, there is often a gap between principle and practice. Some of those who complain about what they see as declining standards are sometimes guilty of some of the very "crimes" against which they protest or of similar ones. The big problem is to determine who would make the most appropriate models for the present day.

According to Allsopp (1972b, 5), a Caribbean community *standard* in the sense of "widest acceptance" by literate persons would more likely be set by its teachers and the *Oxford English Dictionary* than by its politicians, businessmen and journalists. However, it is highly likely that teachers have a less important role as models today, not least because the usage of the other groups mentioned by Allsopp is increasingly placed before the public via newspapers and radio and television stations.

West Indian literature also serves as a guide to the standard, following precedents all over the world. However, the relevant works have usually been subjected to rigorous editing, often carried out by publishers in the United States or Britain. Even so, as more and more writers use Jamaican or other Caribbean settings, some local usage is inevitable. West Indian literature now features prominently in the syllabuses at school and university levels.

One does not have to be a purist to note that the formal spoken and written usage of even well-educated Jamaicans today often includes departures from rules once learned in school. In the areas of morphosyntax and syntax, those departures which are diagnosed as directly reflecting transfer from Creole are least likely to be considered acceptable, for example, absence of inflection on nouns and verbs as well as hypercorrections attributed to persons attempting to avoid Creole. Such occurrences are too frequent to be always, if ever, the fault of the printer's devil. Examples include the following (emphasis added):

1. All major credit and debit *card* accepted. (sign in pharmacy)
2. Police occupy *abandon* houses. (newspaper headline)
3. Our tears *flows*. (item in newspaper)

To the extent that such usage is seen as reflecting an incomplete grasp of the traditional standard, it is not likely to be accepted in either speech or writing at the formal level.

Certain other departures from the traditional norm, however, appear to indicate growing trends in English generally. One such is the tendency to make verbs agree in number with a preceding noun which is not the subject of the sentence but is, rather, part of a phrase which modifies the subject. This happens where the head noun is some distance away from the verb. It occurs in both spoken and written English, as in the following (emphasis added):

1. The police commissioner says the loss of lives *were* regrettable. (radio news)
2. Government clampdown on foreign nationals working in Jamaica without a work permit *have* led to a rush on application renewals. (*Jamaica Observer*)
3. Smoking ganja and other illegal drugs *are* prohibited. (public sign)

Similar examples have been observed in British English. They include the following (emphasis added):

1. The number of attacks on ethnic minorities *soar*. (*Times* online)
2. It is still not clear what the normal sequence of events *are*. (science programme on BBC Radio)

English in Jamaica is also said to be under threat today from another point of view. The call by some linguists and others for Creole to be recognized as a national language has been misinterpreted in some quarters as a call for it to replace English altogether. As a result of this misinterpretation, most of the recent contributions on language to Jamaican newspapers have stressed the perceived limitations or otherwise of Creole, rather than the state of English as such.

The sharp distinction made so far in this chapter between Jamaican English and Jamaican Creole disguises the fact that in practice there is often no clear distinction between them. And highly educated Jamaicans using a form of Standard English on formal occasions does not preclude their speaking or writing something different in other circumstances. Code mixing, the insertion of stereotypical Creole features into formal usage, has also been ignored here so far because it is easily recognized as such and is generally considered acceptable. It most often involves no more than the insertion of a Creole word or phrase for a special effect, as in the following sentence from a columnist writing about American foreign policy in the *Jamaica Observer*: "In addition to the attempt to subvert the law, the Bush administration has openly attempted to *samfi* the world into believing all sorts of impossible things" (John Maxwell, *Jamaica Observer,* 17 September 2006; emphasis added).

The word *samfi*, usually spelled s-a-m-f-i-e, is used here as a verb meaning "to trick". It appears in both Cassidy and Le Page's *Dictionary of Jamaican English* (1980) and Allsopp's *Dictionary of Caribbean English Usage* (1996). This writer used it to signal his shared identity with his fellow Jamaicans. That his choice was deliberate is clearly brought out by the fact that he was discussing American foreign policy, not a specifically Jamaican or Caribbean subject, where its use would have been more predictable.

Despite the absence here of expressed opinions from other parts of the anglophone Caribbean concerning the current state of English, there is good reason to assume that there are many similarities between the actual situation in these countries today and the situation in Jamaica. All are, or have been, British colonies, with all that this entails for the traditional functions and status of English, as well as for the kind of English that has traditionally been promoted. In most cases, as in Jamaica, political independence from Britain has been achieved during the past fifty years, and it was immediately preceded and followed by increased consciousness of a national identity, with linguistic as well as social consequences. The growing influence of American English in recent decades is also a significant factor throughout the Caribbean, for the same reasons as in Jamaica.

Some of the phonological features reported here for formal Jamaican English are also evident at the same level in other parts of the region. They include substitution of alveolar stops for interdental fricatives, metathesis in, for example, the word *ask* and reduction of word-final consonants.

Recognized differences in pronunciation across the anglophone Caribbean include rhoticity in Barbados and to a lesser extent in Guyana and Jamaica versus its absence in Trinidad and other islands with a history of lexically French Creole.

In some of these latter cases, too, although not in Trinidad, the interdental fricatives of British Standard English are usually replaced by /f/ and /v/, a change which has also been reported for Barbados (Roberts 1988, 92).

Barbadians are reputedly the best users of English in the Caribbean. This reputation is largely based on the fact that even usage in Barbados that is furthest removed from Standard English is much closer to it than what would be found in Jamaica or Guyana, for example. Barbadian students perform better than others in English language examinations at the regional level. It was therefore surprising to find an article in a Barbados newspaper (*Nation*, 2 August 2006) which stated that, according to the chief education officer, Barbadians were not achieving an acceptable standard in the acquisition of language skills and that this was partly blamed on the negative influence of Creole.[6] However, the formal usage of educated Barbadians does not appear to have come under public scrutiny to date.

Dominica, St Lucia, Grenada, St Vincent and Tobago were all under French control for varying lengths of time before becoming British colonies. These islands have consequently, like Trinidad, had a history of lexically French Creole, which is still the most widely used vernacular in Dominica and St Lucia today.

Although a lexically French Creole is still the first language of a large proportion of the population of both these islands, in recent decades more and more persons have become bilingual in it and an English vernacular. The latter is not considered a Creole, although it includes calques on the lexically French Creole with which it coexists. It is popularly referred to as English, but studies have shown that teachers, at least, are aware of the contrast between it and the Standard English that is officially promoted in the classroom and elsewhere. When questioned, however, they claimed to value the latter more highly in the classroom.[3] This response most likely reflects their awareness that this is the official target in the school setting, rather than their own competence or their consistent usage in that setting.

Once again, acceptance of new forms and structures is complicated by the fact that they are often diagnosed as examples of interference from Creole. Nevertheless, some changes which are now stigmatized are likely to become accepted in the standard language in the future, and others will inevitably drop out. This has happened several times elsewhere.

Acceptance of change is not a recipe for anarchy. Nor is it being suggested here that change should be actively encouraged. The recent recognition of different standard Englishes in many parts of the world outside of the Caribbean is proof that the definition of standard languages already allows more grammatical variation than in the past. Besides, as Melchers and Shaw (2003, 35) have pointed out, the notion that a uniform and well-regulated standard language code is normal and natural is an illusion which is likely to be less easy to maintain in the future, as electronic media tend to destandardize English and other languages. As long as the different standard languages remain mutually comprehensible, however, there should not be a major problem. Americans and

Englishmen have had no difficulty understanding each other, despite differences in their respective standard languages.

The answer to the question "Whither English in the Caribbean?" is that English is here to stay. Regardless of any structural changes it may have undergone in this setting, or any that it may undergo in the future, it will continue to be a very important means of communication within each of the relevant societies and also, of necessity, the language of international communication.

Notes

1. See letter from Hugh Levy, "The Assassination of English", *Gleaner*, 27 July 1994; letter from Alicia Smith, "Slaughtering the English Language", *Jamaica Observer*, 11 November 2004.
2. Words and symbols enclosed in diagonal slashes follow the phonemic spelling used in Cassidy and Le Page (1980).
3. See Bryan and Burnette (2006) for Dominica and Simmons-McDonald (2006) for St Lucia.

References

Allsopp, Richard. 1972a. *Why a Dictionary of Caribbean English Usage?* Cave Hill: University of the West Indies.

———. 1972b. "The Problem of Acceptability in Caribbean Creolized English". Paper presented at the Conference on Creole Languages and Educational Development, University of the West Indies, St Augustine, Trinidad.

———. 1979. "Caribbean English and Our Schools". *Caribbean Journal of Education* 9 (2): 99–110.

———. 1996. *Dictionary of Caribbean English Usage*. Oxford: Oxford University Press.

Bryan, B., and R. Burnette. 2006. "Language Variation in Dominica: Perceptions, Practice and Policies". *Caribbean Journal of Education* 28 (1): 26–50.

Cassidy, Frederic G., and Robert B. Le Page. 1980. *Dictionary of Jamaican English*. Cambridge: Cambridge University Press.

De Camp, David. 1961. "Social and Geographical Factors in Jamaican Dialects". In *Creole Language Studies II: Proceedings of the Conference on Creole Language Studies*, edited by Robert Le Page, 61–84. London: Macmillan.

Hinrich, Lars, and Joseph T. Farquharson, eds. 2011. *Variation in the Caribbean: From Creole Continua to Individual Agency*. Amsterdam: John Benjamins.

Irvine, Alison. 2004. "A Good Command of the English Language: Phonological Variation in the Jamaican Acrolect". *Journal of Creole Language Studies* 19 (1): 41–76.

Melchers, Gunnel, and Philip Shaw. 2003. *World Englishes*. London: Arnold.

Nesfield, J.C. 1912. *Modern English Grammar*. London: Macmillan.

Roberts, Peter. 1988. *West Indians and Their Language*. Cambridge: Cambridge University Press.

Sand, Andrea. 2011. "Language Attitudes and Linguistic Awareness in Jamaican English". In *Variation in the Caribbean. From Creole Continua to Individual Agency* edited by Lars Hinrich and Joseph T. Farquharson, 163–87. Amsterdam: John Benjamins.

Simmons-McDonald, H. 2006. "Attitudes of Teachers to St Lucian Varieties". *Caribbean Journal of Education* 28 (1): 51–77.

Part 2

Creole Linguistics in the Caribbean

Chapter 2

THE CREOLE CONCEPT IN CULTURE STUDIES

A Revaluation

Mervyn C. Alleyne

The concept of Creole is very difficult to pin down. Even within the same discipline, it has defied definition in spite of sustained efforts. Thus in linguistics, both rationalist-based theories and empirically based theories have failed to account for all Creole phenomena and to exclude non-Creole phenomena. Is Bajan a Creole? Or are the vernaculars of the British and American Virgin Islands Creole? A vacuous question because we do not really know what a Creole is. Some scholars have been carried away by the attractiveness of the term and apply the Creole tag to all Caribbean language phenomena that do not conform to the standard norm. Thus the popular vernacular of Puerto Rico has been called a Spanish Creole, and that of Trinidad, an English Creole. Beyond linguistics, as we will see, it means different things in different parts of the Americas. But the most we can say is that it is very "New World", one of the many cultural products that the New World has given to global human society. It is now used in many disciplines. Outside linguistics, M.G. Smith was one of the early scholars attracted by the term, and he used it in the title of one of his works: *Pluralism, Politics and Ideology in the Creole Caribbean*. This juxtaposition of Creole and pluralism may seem strange because in one of its meanings, Creole is antithetical to pluralism. But Smith, it seems, was merely using a convenient term to refer to one of two cultural zones which emerge from a classification of the Caribbean. Smith does not provide an argument that establishes criteria for such classification. The nearest he comes is when he says, "Most Caribbean societies fall historically and sociologically into two distinct groupings, the Hispanic and the non-Hispanic . . . Given the divergent political, cultural and economic condition and histories of the Hispanic and non-Hispanic Caribbean or Creole societies, in my usage, it is appropriate to consider the latter by themselves" (Smith 1991, 10).

This is indeed a very useful and insightful distinction. But it is a broad generalization. As we understand the Caribbean, we may be able to construct a finer analysis that would, for example, try to account for the complexity of the north Caribbean zone of Colombia, which is more mixed than Barbados and Jamaica and has a so-called Creole language, although the term *criollo* there retains its early meaning of "person of European descent born in the New World". We could account for the similarity in ideology and socioeconomic history between the French and the Hispanic Caribbean. Is it purely accidental that the remaining dependent or colonial territories are French (the French Antilles) and Hispanic (Puerto Rico)? We definitely need to deal with the difficulty of placing Trinidad where there is a contestation over what constitutes the national culture and national ideology.

I wish to claim that the concept of Creole is ill-defined, variable and complex, although it is very appealing both as a concept to express the distinctiveness of Caribbean culture and as a window which allows us to see into the future direction of world society – for example, whether phenotype will replace monolithic race; whether plural identities will be the norm, leading to absence of identity, leading in praxis to no identity and no ethnic strife, all of which are features of the Creole concept. This window may be an illusion because there are other signs, signs of the strengthening of ethnic and national identities leading to conflict. Italy, Germany and other European nations are becoming quite afraid that they may lose their identity under the wave of pluralism sweeping their countries.

Some rather interesting questions arise from the semantic history of the word. If it is true, and it seems logical, that the first meaning of the word *Creole* was "person of European descent born in the New World" and that it later applied to any biological species, including Africans, born in the New World, then one must ask: why would Europeans call African slaves by the same name as themselves? This is strange in light of the fact that Europeans largely reserved for themselves the prerogative of naming groups of people, using, for example, the terms *negro*, *mulatto* and *mestizo* (all loaded with pejorative connotations) and *indio* (a gross geographical error which we have perpetuated), as well as assigning their personal names to their slave property. They also created a number of antitheses related to the prototypical contrast of black and white. This prerogative was a major instrument of control for setting the semantic and symbolic norms which would underlie the operations of these New World societies and indeed of the world – consider the Middle East, the Far East and the Mediterranean.

In trying to understand, without fully explaining it, why the regime of slavery, which would seem to contradict the use of the same name for master and slave, would allow the terms *criollo* and *Creole* to be used for both whites and blacks, we should note that slavery was not the initial form of society, or at least not the only one. Early post-Columbian Caribbean societies have been divided historically into two main types: *société d'habitation*, typical of the Hispanic societies, and *société de plantation*, which developed later. This division has been quite significant and heuristic in explaining some of the variations in Caribbean societies and cultures and supports the classification posed by M.G. Smith. In the *société d'habitation*, economic production was based on small, undercapitalized holdings requiring relatively small volumes of manpower which could be acquired from several sources, not only from Africa; whereas the plantation required larger volumes of manpower which was sought from Africa. But some colleagues and myself have recently proposed a third type (existing earlier than the *société d'habitation* and continuing in some places up to present day, side-by-side with the other, better-known systems), which we are calling "*société de co-habitation*". The *société de co-habitation* focuses on the role of a marginalized majority in shaping language, culture and identity. It ascribes agency to peoples of African descent, indigenous peoples and marginalized people of European descent, who had their own political, economic and cultural agendas: buccaneers, privateer communities in Hispaniola, Tortuga and on the Caribbean coast of Central America, and Maroon communities everywhere, Black Caribs and Black Seminoles.

The other consideration which I wish to propose is that the designation of slaves born in the New World as *criollo* was not motivated so much by their relations with Europeans as by the need to separate them from slaves or Africans in general born in Africa. This latter need must have been overwhelming and compelling enough to have superseded the need to distinguish between Europeans and Africans in general. It would then be the beginning of a continuing effort and strategy to counter the perceived threat of an African identity and replace it with a New World identity, thereby splitting the African community in two. The Creole phenomenon was well under way.

As a concept, and as a process which continues to underlie theories of Caribbean culture, the term *Creole* was never until now used in the English colonial Caribbean, either in popular discourse or in scientific discourse. In the French colonial Caribbean, the term belongs firmly to popular discourse; it has crept into the scientific discourse where, as we would expect of the French tradition, it has received the most explicit elaborate theoretical treatment (*Eloge de la créolité* [Bernabé, Chamoiseau and Confiant 1993]). The Hispanic zone is where it has remained closest to its early or earliest meaning. This is especially true of South America, whereas in the Hispanic Caribbean, the term *criollo* has a variety of meanings, with the dominant corresponding variable being social class. Persons of the upper class use "criollo" in its early meaning; the other classes use it to refer to their ethnic and national identity. In Puerto Rico, it is used in this way, but rather infrequently compared with the preferred term *Boricua*. "Criollo" then is used mainly to refer to a kind of cuisine.

I shall now summarize a selected group of Caribbean territories in terms of the way in which the Creole concept is constructed.

Trinidad. The term *Creole* is used chiefly in relation to a former ethnic group made up of the descendants of French colonists. They are recognized primarily by their French names coupled with high social status. Its use here is a continuation of the earliest meaning: "person of European descent born in the New World". Trinidad also continues the early semantic expansion of the term to refer to "any biological species raised in the New World" (Allsopp 1996, 177). It was widely used to distinguish locally bred horses from the thoroughbreds, as well as local poultry ("common fowl" as we called it) from the imported thoroughbreds. This meaning is fading, especially in urbanized Trinidad, where the experience of these species is chiefly from the supermarket shelves or TV cartoons. The French-based vernacular, called "Creole" in the linguistics literature, is called "patois" by its diminishing group of speakers. As the French-based high-status group fades as a distinct ethnic group – the ethnic institutions such as clubs and football teams no longer existing – the meaning "local" with some implication of "mixed" dominates, together with a growing assertion of a dominant African input into the Creole identity. In Trinidad, as well as in Barbados, an Africa-based identity and ideology is only now strengthening largely due to the need felt by this segment of the population for an historical identity to match the strong historically based ethnicity of the Indo group. Trinidadians, like their brothers in the United States, are struggling to find an appropriate term to represent their new ethnic awareness and many still resist the terms *black* and *African*. For them, *Creole* is a more acceptable term. The meaning of Creole also contains an element of sensuality. The widest areas of its use are in "Creole food" and "Creole bacchanal", in reference to the carnival celebration. But here too, the term may be referring to the historical link of the French Creoles to the event.

Martinique. In spite of the influence of Aimé Césaire, the Creole ideology has dominated Martiniquan thinking and awareness, and here the term *Creole* means "mixed"; when interpreted within the postmodern theories of identity, it also means rejection of essentialist notions of origins, rejection of polarities and acceptance of an "in-betweenness" which is constantly redefining itself. The major work *Eloge de la créolité* has no parallel in the anglophone Caribbean.

Puerto Rico. It has a national ideology of homogeneity, and it rejects cultural pluralism. There is no threat from an Africa-based identity because persons of African descent also generally accept the ideology of homogeneity. Posing no threat, Africa can then be romanticized, as is the *indio*, as something of the past which has enriched the now homogeneous Puerto Rican culture. As with everywhere in the Caribbean, ambiguity and ambivalence reign, a double consciousness often expressed as a distinction between public and private behaviour. Ninety per cent of Puerto Ricans check "white" when asked about their racial classification on forms such as for passports and censuses; yet some recent research claims that 70 per cent of Puerto Ricans have indigenous female mitochondrial DNAs (Martínez-Cruzado et al. 2001, 491, 492).

Jamaica. *Black* is the national ideology, but ambivalence prevails. Africa is a major component of blackness, supported historically by the Maroons and currently by the Rastafarian movement. *Maroon* is an unbroken line of consciousness of Africa; and *Rastafarianism* is a recreation of consciousness inspired opportunistically by the coincidental conjuncture of Marcus Garvey and Haile Selassie. The word *Creole* is not used, nor is Creole a concept. But the ruling class's ideal is expressed in the motto "Out of many, one people", which might suggest a recognition of the Creole concept, but the motto is often mockingly reacted to with the query: "One people? Yes. But *which* one?", suggesting a pluralism dominated by one of the competing groups.

In summary, the term *Creole* belongs to a long list of expressions in human language, in this case the languages of the colonial powers that controlled the destiny of the Caribbean in the post-Columbian era. These languages reflect the appropriation by the powerful of the prerogative of naming and thereby of setting the semantic norms of the experience of the powerless. The major instrument of this process is the imposition of the language of the powerful, with all its historically built-in semantic structures favouring its culture (values, world view, etc.). In the same way that colours which are used to represent the major "races" have developed pejorative connotations (in the case of *black*, *red* and *yellow*) and ameliorative connotations (in the case of *white*), so too has the vocabulary representing the ecology and ethnicity/culture of the peoples of the world. Two outstanding examples are the connotations of *jungle* and *tribe*. These words in English (and their counterparts in other European languages) now connote (and may even denote) wild, uncontrolled disorder. In Jamaica, as elsewhere, the expression "law of the jungle" refers to uncontrolled anarchy, with everybody, man and beast, free to roam about hurting one another. This is far from the real state of a jungle in its pristine form, where a very clear natural order exists in which, for example, killing takes place for the purpose of satisfying hunger and in self-defence. Unmotivated, senseless acts of conflict and slaughter between and among men and beasts are not at all typical of the jungle. Such acts are, in fact, more typical of "civilized" cities and countries.

The word *tribe* and its other western European cognates come from the Latin *tribus*, which originally had a neutral referential application. It referred to divisions of the Roman population (e.g., *tribus urbana*, the city group; *tribus rustica*, country folk). The word *tribe* now refers chiefly to African, Asian and indigenous American ethnic groups, seen as still in a precivilized, "savage" state. Thus the Yoruba and the Igbo are "tribes", but the Northern Ireland Catholics and Protestants are "ethnic groups", as are the Serbs and Croats and the Basques and Catalans.

In Jamaica, in a particularly insensitive usage, ultrapartisan politics is referred to as "tribal politics", and the political parties so engaged are called tribes.

However, these are not the only cases. European languages are replete with cases of positive denotations/connotations associated with words expressing aspects of European ecology and culture, and negative ones associated with words expressing other ecologies and cultures. Compare, for example, the words *classical, modern* and *civilized* with the words *traditional, folk, savage* and *primitive*. *Savage* is ultimately from the Latin *silvaticus* (or its colloquial variant, *salvaticus*), meaning "of the forest". In English, its etymological denotative meaning is now subordinate to its connotative expansion: "wild", "ruthless", "cruel". Its nearer antecedent is the French *sauvage*, which in one of its meanings – "uncultivated" – retains part of the Latin denotation. In French, *un arbre sauvage* is a "tree growing in the wild", one which has not been planted by humans. This meaning has been completely lost in English.

Even the words *clothed* and *naked* no longer have merely simple denotative meanings but contain connotations of decency and morality and indecency and immorality, respectively. This particularly hurts the evaluation of some groups living in equatorial climates, where it is more natural and sensible for the body not to be covered (either by hair or by clothes), as indeed it may be more natural and sensible there for the skin to contain high proportions of melanin and for noses to be wide and flat. In addition to a racial hierarchy, we now have in today's world what may be referred to as a hierarchy of cultures.

The term *Creole* is historically part of this process of control through language. It was coined because in the colonization of the New World, it was in the interests of the powerful to make and impose a distinction between persons born in the homeland and those born in the colonies. These latter had already begun to show cultural differences which were negatively valued and later began to show a diminished loyalty to the land of their forefathers and to act in their local interests rather than in the interests of the homeland. Later, the term was conveniently used to make and impose another distinction important to the powerful, the distinction between slaves born in Africa and those born in the colonies.

This creation of different rival groups within the ranks of the powerless is a well-known device of control utilized by colonial powers. It is the origin of the negative evaluation of things African and the continuing desire by the descendants of Africans to distance themselves in every respect from things African, be it phenotype or culture. *Black* and *African* became, and still are, expressions that connote this devaluation; *white*, *Creole* and *brown* came to connote higher value. To say that you spoke Creole or patois was a notch above speaking an African language, even though Creole and patois were held in contempt by the powerful, who then succeeded in passing on this contempt to the speakers of these languages. This is the sad tragedy of the colonial syndrome. This same syndrome is reported for South Africa where, according to one scholar, "the specifying and naming of African speech forms by missionaries in such a way as to suggest differences between them which then were presented also as ethnic boundaries were 'linguistic inventions . . . structured in such a way as to encourage Africans to internalize European epistemology about themselves'". Similarly, in the Caribbean, the speech of slaves (as well as their culture and general behaviour) was viewed as a dichotomy between African languages and Creole or patois and between these latter and "English". It is probable however that, rather than a discrete language, the speech of slaves resembled a chain that "offers a choice of varieties and registers in the speakers' immediate environment" (Fardon and Furniss 1994, 4). For example, the Coromanti language of Jamaican Maroons seems to be closer to the rural form of Jamaican Creole than this Creole is to English. This allows us to adjust the structure of the Jamaican language and culture continuum by placing Coromanti language and religion, and I am sure Coromanti music, at one pole. Alleyne (1971, 174, 175) has already proposed that the Creole continuum is not a contemporary phenomenon but goes back to the very inception of slave societies in the Americas.

The Creole phenomenon, as I have already suggested, whether in language, phenotype, biology or social psychology, served as a refuge for those who wished to distance themselves from things African. This continues up to today and is embraced everywhere in the Caribbean as a positive focus of identity.

The term *Creole* is gaining further currency, spreading to areas such as literary criticism and all the other areas of art and to sociology and political science discourses on identity. It is particularly attractive to, and widely used by, postmodernism, a current philosophical and literary movement. Several postmodern interests seem to coincide with features of the Creole concept. First of all, Creole is linked to the central postmodern discourse on hybridity. And by the way, as I hinted at the beginning, hybridity does not seem to match well with pluralism, although it has to be admitted that it is not clear whether hybridity is an empirical structural feature of contemporary society or whether it is an idealism waiting to be achieved. In any case, hybridity seems to be a universal in the history of human society. At different periods of human history, hybridization (or creolization if you wish) has become another purity, another essence – somewhere in the future the *dougla* of Trinidad may come to be seen as a pure race, and *brown* as phenotype may come to replace *black* and *white* as the purest essence of humanity.

Second, Creole languages are considered to oppose the "meta or master narratives" of linguistic science. They do not have a single parent; in fact their ancestry is shrouded in uncertainty and they are much more "hybrid" than "pure". In many respects Creole languages defy the authoritative definitions in linguistic science. An essential characteristic of Creole language, music, food and culture in general is considered to be eclectivism and syncretism, combining forms from different sources. This is a general feature of the Caribbean even where the term *Creole* is not used to refer to the phenomenon. Caribbean religions such as Vodou, Shango and Revival are considered syncretic, and even the very recent Rastafarianism is seen as combining Judaism, Christianity, Islam, Hinduism, Garvey philosophy and Jamaican traditional culture. Creole languages (at least some of them) are considered to have blurred boundaries, ambiguity and considerable simultaneity, all being basic tenets of postmodern literary and cultural theory. It should be pointed out, however, that blurred boundaries are not an idiosyncratic feature of Creole languages (or cultures) but are quite general. In some views, "language", or rather "speech", is not a discrete, homogeneous, bounded and "boxed" unit but a "multilayered" and partially connected chain. In fact, the very notion of languages as discrete units, or "boxes", is a product of European positivism.

The Creole concept therefore is full of ambiguity and the attitudes towards it are similarly ambiguous, at once positive and negative. The positive attitudes stem from an affective attachment to the language, music, cuisine and phenotype as "ours" – in other words, it is what makes us who we are. The other main attractive feature of Creole, both to locals and foreigners, is its evocation of sensuality (music, dance, cuisine) and, to locals, its honesty (language). In some contexts, the use of the standard language is associated with duplicity and insincerity, whereas the Creole language is associated with honesty and straightforwardness (Alleyne 1961; Rickford and Traugott 1985).

I have always favoured the principle of designating these Caribbean vernaculars in terms of the adjective of nationality of their speakers: Jamaican, Haitian, Guyanese and so forth. This principle is best observed and implemented in cases in which the language is standardized and has become an official language of a nation, as is the case with Haitian. But it is also relevant in cases where a people takes consciousness of its worth and, as it emerges from a period of colonialism, begins the process of the revalorization of its language and culture. Its language becomes a strong symbol of its national identity. So why use the designation *Jamaican* rather than *Creole*? To answer this question, we may consider a psychological and epistemological progression that colonized countries undergo:

1. The Western world establishes the semantic norms through naming and value assignments.
2. European modalities become the norm and all other manifestations are judged in relation to these norms.
3. Colonial peoples accept them and undervalue their own cultural productions.
4. Postcolonial reactions attempt to revalorize these productions, which then require renaming.

Countries, cities, streets, individuals and so on are renamed. African Americans and indigenous peoples of the Americas are engaged in a long journey to find appropriate names for themselves. Linton Kwesi Johnson, the leading exponent of the genre *dub*, now finds the term limiting: "I consider myself a poet, full stop" (Johnson 2006). He sees *dub* as another example of denying non-Western cultural productions their rightful place in the universal order. This order makes Christianity a religion but Vodou a cult; Northern Irish Catholics and Protestants are ethnic groups, whereas the Ibo and the Yoruba are tribes; Western music, medicine, art and so on are full representatives of the universal canon requiring no restrictive epithet, whereas non-Western forms are "ethnic" (cf. "ethno-medicine", "ethno-music"). The terms *Creole* and *patois* belong to the same category as *indio*, *negro*, *mulatto* and *coolie*.

Finally, there are several currents criss-crossing over human society at the present time, in some cases mutually reinforcing, in other cases conflicting and paradoxical. For example, there is, of course, globalization, the free movement of capital accompanied by the free or forced movement of people. On the one hand, this produces new configurations of heterogeneity and pluralism; but on the other hand, it is leading to a levelling of cultural differences and a borderless seamless modernity. For some peoples it is producing multiple identities or even no identity, with anomie as its social pathological expression; for others it is enhancing ethnic identity as a defence against social and economic marginalization, perceived or real. Can the outcomes of these currents be subsumed under the rubric "Creole" or "creolization"?

Trinidad is perhaps the best Caribbean example of the direction that world culture may be taking. In Trinidad, ethnic groups are still vying either for supremacy or for survival, maintaining or creating identities – some stronger than others, many with no ethnic identity at all (e.g., the *dougla*). At the same time, a national identity is emerging, creating multiple identities. The group that is making the biggest claim as the foundation of national identity is the one with the weakest ethnic identity, the Creole group. It will be interesting to see whether this group triumphs eventually, with other ethnic groups accepting what may become a new hegemony.

Throughout the Caribbean, a major problem is what will be the fate of the black group, which is now somewhat absorbed into the larger potpourri Creole group. Mixed societies, multiple identities or no identity in a Creole world may be a thing of the future and may even be the best for the world, hopefully with erasure of traditional locations of power. But right now what is needed most is the elevation and revaluation of the cultural behaviour, and a positive strengthening of the ethnicity of the black populations: proper schools and other education opportunities, government services treating them equally; respect for their language; the significant symbols and the iconography lauding thick lips and flat noses and extreme melanin. Only when these psychosocial reforms have been made will be able to talk about Creole identity or mixed identity or no identity at all.

References

Alleyne, Mervyn. 1961. "Language and Society in St. Lucia". *Caribbean Studies* 1 (1): 1–10.

———. 1971. "Acculturation and the Cultural Matrix of Creolization". In *Pidginization and Creolization of Languages*, edited by Dell Hymes, 169–86. Cambridge: Cambridge University Press.

Allsopp, Richard. 1996. *Dictionary of Caribbean English Usage*. Oxford: Oxford University Press.

Bernabé, Jean, Patrick Chamoiseau and Raphaël Confiant. *Éloge de la créolité*. Paris: Gallimard, 1993.

Fardon, Richard, and Graham Furniss, eds. 1994. *African Languages, Development and the State*. London: Routledge.

Johnson, Linton Kwesi. 2006. *Mi Revalueshanary Fren*. Port Townsend, WA: Ausuble.

Martínez-Cruzado, J.C., G. Toro-Labrador, V. Ho-Fung and M. Estevez-Montero. 2001. "Mitochondrial DNA Analysis Reveals Substantial Native American Ancestry in Puerto Rico". *Human Biology*, August, 73–74.

Rickford, John R., and Elizabeth C. Traugott. 1985. "Symbol of Powerlessness and Degeneracy, or Symbol of Solidarity and Truth? Paradoxical Attitudes Toward Pidgins and Creoles". In *The English Language Today*, edited by Sidney Greenbaum, 252–61. Oxford: Pergamon.

Smith, M.G. 1991. *Pluralism, Politics and Ideology in the Creole Caribbean*. Vera Rubin Caribbean Series. New York: Research Institute of the Study of Man.

Chapter 3

REDUPLICATION AND LANGUAGE CHANGE IN GUYANA

Alim Hosein

Introduction

More than half a century ago, Richard Allsopp recognized the existence of varieties in Guyanese language use which could be arranged in the manner of a continuum from the most English-like to the least English-like. This insight was later developed by others into the notion of a "Creole continuum". It also featured in formulating the concept of "decreolization", a process summed up by Seigel (2008, 236) as "the gradual modification of a creole in the direction of the lexifier". One theoretical implication of decreolization is that the Creole could eventually disappear. Decreolization has become a classic concept in Caribbean Creoles with Guyanese Creole English (hereafter, GY) identified as one language that is said to be in the process of decreolizing.

Guyana is described as an English-speaking country, with English listed as the official language. However, there have been significant social, economic and cultural developments in Guyana, especially since independence in 1966, which have created among the population a growing sense of security and comfort with things Guyanese. Thus, popular culture is overwhelmingly conducted in varieties of Creole, but Creole varieties also seem to have penetrated official circles. Also, the rise of what is called "international English" or "world English" has given the Guyanese further confidence to speak their own versions of English. The emergence of Guyanese diasporas has also helped the Guyanese to see themselves as international people who are comfortable in their own skin.

This interaction or side-by-side existence of official and popular cultures, with speakers moving in a fluid, nondiglossic environment, creates a language situation which is not easy to characterize by the straightforward continuum model. Thus, although Allsopp's observation remains valid fifty years on, there is scope for the further examination of Creole life-cycle concepts such as "decreolization". A question that could be asked about the contemporary language situation in Guyana is whether there truly is a loss of Creole elements in a one-way movement from Creole to English.

Why was reduplication chosen for this study? As a linguistic strategy through which meaning is expressed, reduplication is used to create lexical or grammatical forms which parallel forms or functions in English. While much work has been done on reduplication in Caribbean creoles, the focus has been on its semantics, phonology and grammar. I hypothesize that language change along the decreolization model will result in reduplicated forms in GY being replaced by forms from English.

Reduplication

Generally, reduplications are repetitions of words or parts of words – for example, *run run, lef lef* and *one one* – to signal a lexical or grammatical function. There are also repeated reduplications, for example, *taak taak taak taak, trembly trembly trembly trembly, run run run run*.

Although reduplication is found in many creole languages, be they English, Dutch, Spanish or French, the phenomenon is not restricted to these kinds of languages because there are many non-Creoles (e.g., Sanskrit, Turkish) in which reduplication and partial reduplication play major grammatical roles. Some linguists see reduplication as a defining feature of Creole morphology, whereas other linguists do not. Parkvall (2000, 80) for example, casts some doubts on the currency of reduplication in Creoles when he says that "in many Atlantic Creoles, reduplication is no longer productive, and one can only speculate whether or not what must etymologically be seen as reduplicative structures are synchronically opaque fossilised remnants of a former morphological process".

English, which is the official language in Guyana, also evidences reduplications, but these are of kinds which are either not attested in, or are not very productive in, GY. Reduplication in English is notably discursive – that is, it is used for contrastive, deprecative, rhyming and other discourse functions. These, with few exceptions, do not occur in GY, as shown in table 3.1.

GY also has a significant number of what Kouwenberg and LaCharité (2001a) call "pseudo-reduplications" – forms such as *ning ning* (being caught in a bind; to be in deep trouble) and *poto poto* (soft mud), which may have come directly from substrate languages such as Akan and Ijo or from Hindi/Bhojpuri (e.g., *chul chul, puunch paanch, labr labr, cha cha, nana*). Pseudo-reduplications resemble reduplications, but have no semantically related uniterated base form (**ning*; **poto*).

Although Kouwenberg and LaCharité (2001a) make a strong and persuasive argument against the inclusion of such forms under the rubric "reduplication", I include them as one aspect of this study because my focus is on speakers' continued knowledge and use of forms that arose out of the creolization process. Like true reduplications, they also establish a pattern of repetition within a word, which is not typical in English.

Table 3.1. Comparison of Guyanese and English types of reduplication

	English	Guyanese
Contrastive	Did you SEE him see him?	–
Partial	Hap-happy	–
Deprecative	Work-smork	–
Rhyming	Real-deal	–
Ablaut	Riff-raff	e.g., Bip bap
Baby talk	Wa-wa	e.g., Din din
Intensive	Many many	e.g., Nuff nuff

Source: Based on Ghomeshi et al. 2004, 309.

Pseudo-reduplications are typically lexical in function – they name things, events and states – as opposed to true reduplications, which can be lexical but can also serve grammatical functions.

The Research

The purpose of the research was, first, to identify the extent of reduplication use in samples of the Guyanese population and, second, to examine the integration of reduplication in message creation in GY.

The central data collection points were the University of Guyana (UG) campuses in Berbice (sixty-four persons), sixty miles away from the capital city of Georgetown, and in Turkeyen, which is five miles outside the capital city. At Turkeyen, data were collected from students (forty persons) and also from visitors to campus during an annual Open Day exercise (eighteen persons). These three collections yielded respondents who live in differing communities and who were also of different ages, ethnicities, occupations, levels of education and other social variables.

In the research, a list of reduplications (including pseudo-reduplications) was created and tested among different groups of persons to ascertain the authenticity of the reduplications. This list was shown to two other groups (the Berbice and Open Day groups) who were asked to indicate whether they knew and used the different reduplications. These exercises gave an insight into the currency of reduplication in GY. Then the list was read to a third group (Turkeyen) who simultaneously indicated reduplications which they knew and which they knew and would use. To add another layer of insight to the research, the variables of *age* and *attitude towards English and GY* were added to the data collected from this third group.

A third level of data collection took the form of recording actually-occurring reduplications from the radio, television and newspapers and from Guyanese in their normal interactions with others, to supplement the elicited data with actual reduplications.

Use of Reduplications

Although in all the groups more persons reported knowing reduplications rather than using them and some reduplications were more well known and well used than others, there was a healthy attestation of knowledge and use of reduplication among all the respondents. In the data from the Open Day group, eleven respondents (61.1 per cent) reported knowledge and use of at least one-third of the reduplications listed, with some persons claiming to recognize and use as many as forty-seven of the fifty-one reduplications. The Berbice group reported the most consistently high knowledge and use of reduplications, judging not only by the high percentage (forty-six of the sixty-four persons: 71.8 per cent) who claimed to know and use the reduplications, but also by the small differential between the highest (forty-seven) and lowest numbers of reduplications (thirty) that most persons claimed to know and use. In this group, only eleven respondents reported knowing and using fewer than seventeen of the reduplications.

The Turkeyen group showed positive indications in all the age groups (see sample in table 3.2).

The research also shows that pseudo-reduplications are recognized and used by many of the respondents. Reports of awareness and use were high in all three groups, but the Berbice group showed higher scores for reduplications like *chul chul* and *moco moco*, which showed relatively low scores in the other two groups. At Turkeyen, even among the younger students (ages 17–20), there is significant knowledge and also use of pseudo-reduplications, although these are lower than among the older groups.

Results of the survey of attitude towards English and GY (table 3.4) show that although most of the students had a healthy respect for Creole, most of them saw themselves as speaking more English than Creole some or most of the time. Most of them also saw themselves as "modern" people. Yet the bias towards English does not preclude significant knowledge and usage of reduplication by these respondents. Their self-perception as "modern" persons seems to reside comfortably alongside their use of reduplication.

Table 3.2. Knowledge and use of reduplications – Turkeyen group (students)

Age range & no. of persons	Know						Use					
	17–20 (7)	21–25 (11)	26–30 (10)	31–40 (7)	41–50 (5)	Total (40)	17–20 (7)	21–25 (11)	26–30 (10)	31–40 (7)	41–50 (5)	Total (40)
Brukup brukup	5	8	8	6	5	**32**	4	6	5	1	4	**20**
Holey holey	6	9	10	6	5	**36**	5	7	7	5	5	**29**
Back back	3	7	7	7	5	**29**	1	6	5	2	5	**19**
Saafy saafy	5	9	6	6	4	**30**	5	7	6	6	3	**27**
Big big	5	9	7	5	5	**31**	3	6	5	3	4	**21**
Waan waan	6	9	8	5	5	**33**	4	8	8	5	5	**30**
Lef lef	6	9	10	5	5	**35**	3	8	8	5	5	**29**
Anda anda	2	5	2	4	1	**14**	2	2	1	1	0	**6**

Table 3.3. Knowledge and use of pseudo-reduplications – Turkeyen group (students)

Age range & no. of persons	Know						Use					
	17–20 (7)	21–25 (11)	26–30 (10)	31–40 (7)	41–50 (5)	Total	17–20 (7)	21–25 (11)	26–30 (10)	31–40 (7)	41–50 (5)	Total
Chul chul	0	3	1	1	1	6	0	1	1	0	0	2
Kuss kuss	4	7	8	6	5	30	3	6	8	6	5	28
Moco moco	3	9	8	5	4	29	1	5	6	3	4	19
Su su	5	11	9	7	5	37	2	9	10	7	5	33
Bizi bizi	4	11	9	7	5	36	4	11	10	6	5	36

Table 3.4. Attitude to language – Turkeyen group (students)

Age range and no. of persons	17–20 (7)	21–25 (11)	26–30 (10)	31–40 (7)	41–50 (5)
I am old-fashioned.	3	3	0	1	2
I am modern.	3	7	9	4	3
I speak English most of the time	2	3	4	2	3
I speak Creole most of the time.	1	6	1	1	0
I speak English some of the time.	3	2	7	3	2
I speak Creole some of the time.	2	0	1	4	3
Creole must be used as much as English.	3	11	8	3	2

Reduplication in Guyanese

As table 3.5 shows, reduplication in GY can take place in most grammatical categories or word classes, although less so in prepositions.

Table 3.5 shows that reduplication does not simply serve the purpose of translating or copying concepts from English or iconically representing actions and ideas. Such reduplications would have been easy targets of "repair" in the process of decreolization and therefore would be more susceptible to erosion from the language. However, we see language functions continued through reduplication instead of English and the maintenance of a productive lexicon, morphology and semantics through reduplication in GY to meet communicative needs.

Table 3.5. Examples of reduplication in Guyanese Creole

PREP	Under	<u>anda anda</u> biznis	<u>illegal/secretive</u> business/activities
ADJ	Big	he like play <u>big big</u>	he likes to pretend that he is <u>more than he is</u>
	Broken	de fence <u>brukup brukup</u>	The fence is <u>delapidated</u>
ADV	One	me deh <u>waan waan waan waan</u> we use to do art	I am feeling <u>poorly</u> <u>once in a while</u> we used to do art
	Corner	mus waak <u>carna carna</u>	walk on the kerb/walk <u>carefully</u>
	Big	he like taak <u>big big</u>	he likes to <u>brag/talk aggressively</u>
VERB	Asking	stop <u>askin askin</u> question	stop your <u>incessant questioning</u>
	Come	he does <u>come come</u> by me	he <u>visits often/sporadically</u>
	Play	he only <u>a play play</u> dead	he is <u>pretending</u> to be dead
NOUN	Cousin	dem a <u>cousin cousin</u>	they are <u>cousins</u>
	House	dey playin <u>house house</u>	they are playing <u>doll's house</u>

Lexical Functions

Through reduplication, words are created and concepts are encapsulated. The created words do not have the same reference as the original English words. The following are examples:

- Under: *anda anda* – illegal/secretive: *I doan like dem anda anda business*
- Left: *lef lef* – leftovers

- Burn: *bun bun* – burnt food at the bottom of a pot. There is no word for this in English, so this word fills a lexical gap.
- Hide: *hide hide* – code language for covert behaviour; can also refer specifically to illicit sexual encounters. In the former, the reduplication is used as a verb: *dey hide hide and teef de mango*; whereas in the latter, it is a noun: *dey doing hide hide*.

Semantic Functions

a. Reduplication allows different levels of meaning to be encoded:
   - Corner: *carna* – has the same reference as in English. However, when reduplicated, it can convey different meanings:
     waak carna carna can mean both "walk on the kerb/at the very side of the road" and "walk carefully".
   - *pinch pinch* – refers not only to pinching, but also to incessant/repeated pinching.

b. The meanings of words can be semantically extended:
   - Half: *haaf haaf* – distributed in halves: *gi dem haaf haaf banana*; but also *haffa haffa* – weak, incapable, mediocre: *wha kinda haffa haffa man you?*
   - Burn: *bun bun* – burnt food at bottom of pot
   - Speed: *speedy speedy* – suspiciously: *he acting speedy speedy* (he is acting in a suspicious manner)

c. Reduplication facilitates morphology and enables semantic functions which are not possible through English conjugations:
   - Bore (to pierce): bore + y (*bory*) is not attested in GY, but *bory bory* to mean "with many holes" is – *the wall look bory bory*.
   - Soft: *saaf* + y (*saafy*): not found in GY, but *saafy saafy* is – *de rice saufy saufy*.

Morphological Functions

Reduplication is used as a derivational device and so extends the lexicon of the language:
- Girl: *gyurl gyurl* (effeminate)
- Play: *play play* (to pretend)

It is also used as an inflectional device for grammatical purposes:

- Run: *stop run run* (stop the running)

It facilitates multifunctionality:

- Space (N): *the fence spacey spacey* (ADJ)

Direction of Language Change

Reduplicated forms found in GY also show incorporation of elements of English grammar, which suggests that reduplication in the language resists erosion or that the speakers of GY are undergoing a mass interlingual stage in transition from Creole forms to English forms. The second interpretation would yield interlanguage redundancies and ungrammatical forms, but this is not seen in GY reduplication. Some examples of such incorporation are:

a. Addition of inflection
he a pinch pinch/pinch pinchin/pinchin pinchin mi.

This occurs with other punctual verbs (e.g., *jook*), but can also occur with non-punctual verbs:

di bebi a crai crai/crai craiin/craiin craiin.

b. Addition of y on ADJ to indicate attenuation of the ADJ
de rice saafy saafy (versus *de rice saaf saaf*)

c. ADV plus reduplication
she kinda crazy crazy – she is a bit eccentric
de wata lil choppy choppy today – the sea is kind of rough today

d. ADV plus reduplication of ADJ plus -y
it sorta/kinda greeny greeny
it look lil greeny greeny

Everyday Use of Reduplication

For a language form to be considered to be alive, it must show vitality – actual continued use, and application relevant to changing social situations. To ascertain if this is the case in GY, reduplication in everyday GY speech was sought out. The finding is that there is strong evidence of continued and relevant use of reduplications within everyday GY speech. Table 3.6 gives examples of reduplications heard both from Guyanese speakers in actual, natural conversations and from the news media.

The table shows use of reduplication

Table 3.6. Examples of actual reduplications used in Guyana

I playin taxi taxi	Af M 8+, Uitvlugt[1] – when asked what he was doing
Waan waan we use to do art We do waan waan ting	Mx F 18, Better Hope/Industry – during board of studies examination of her art exhibition
Some people tell you some real flighty flighty ting	Af F 20s, University of Guyana undergraduate student – during in-class discussion
. . . and she deh wildy wildy wildy wildy	Host (Af M 30+) in conversation with caller on live interactive television program, *Love and Laughter*, channel 9, 3 July 2010
. . . for different different reasons	Af M 20, University of Guyana undergraduate student – during in-class discussion
It does cook mashup mashup	Af F 30–40, Ann's Grove – during interview, undergraduate linguistics field trip
. . . you can't send any long-long[2] attachment	Prt F 50+, Ogle – NGO administrator to friend on phone complaining about slow Internet service
My head doan work piecy piecy	Af M 60, – University of Guyana lecturer – in bantering exchange with student on campus
Plenty strange strange people livin here now	EI M 70+, Industry – in casual conversation
. . . he was acting "speedy speedy"	*Sunday Stabroek*,[3] 25 April 2010, page 2 – quote from witness in report on a murder in Herstelling, East Bank Demerara
Sealey [. . .] was known for his "speed, speed driving"	*Stabroek News*, 2 July 2010, page 10 – verbatim insert in report on fatal accident, quoting two men from Kwakwani, Berbice

- for a range of functions: metaphor, intensification, gap-filling, distribution, word creation and so on.
- by persons of different ages.
- at different social levels.
- in different social situations.
- in different parts of Guyana.
- by different ethnic groups.

Conclusion

The research strongly suggests that the classic decreolization hypothesis does not hold. Reduplication continues to be a popular, productive and useful linguistic strategy in GY. Speakers of all ages and walks of life use it for discourse regardless of their competence in English. For example, although GY speakers can and do express themselves in the acrolect, they have not lost their use of reduplication and pseudo-reduplications. Reduplication remains an active parallel resource in the oral language of the country, being retained as part of both basilectal language (e.g., *waan waan we use to do art*) and also as part of the acrolect (e.g., *you can't send any long-long attachment*).

There does not seem to be a direction of movement in which reduplication is replaced by English forms. In addition, although some reduplications (e.g., *poto poto*) are not as well known to some younger people, young people do make use of reduplication strategies. Moreover, younger and older persons have extended reduplication strategies to "new" words and experiences (e.g., *he only textin textin me; you got to study study all de time; de place smell KFC KFC*). The frequency of

Table 3.7. Sample of "new" reduplicated words – Turkeyen group (students)

Age range & no. of persons	Use					
	17–20 (7)	20–25 (11)	25–30 (10)	30–40 (7)	40–50 (5)	Total
Textin textin	1	6	4	3	1	15
Study study	3	2	2	2	3	12
KFC KFC	0	2	0	2	1	5
Phone phone	2	2	2	5	2	13
Travel travel	2	3	1	5	2	13

these "new" reduplications is lower than that of the other reduplications, but their existence is significant:

In other words, the strategy of reduplication has not "fossilised" in Guyana, and Guyanese Creole is not marching inexorably to its demise.

Notes

1. Indicates ancestry, gender, age and location: Af = African; Mx = Mixed; Prt = Portuguese; EI = East Indian; M= male; F = female.
2. To be read with falling, then rising intonation (instead of two equal stresses, which would indicate intensification).
3. A major Guyanese newspaper.

References

Bakker, Peter, and Mikael Parkvall. 2005. "Reduplication in Pidgins and Creoles". In *Studies on Reduplication*, edited by Bernard Hurch, 511–32. Berlin: Mouton de Gruyter.
Devonish, Hubert. 2003. "Reduplication as Lexical and Syntactic Aspect Marking: The Case of Guyanese Creole". In *Twice as Meaningful: Reduplication in Pidgins, Creoles and Other Contact Languages*, edited by Silvia Kouwenberg, 47–60. London: Battlebridge.
Ghomeschi, J., R. Jackendoff, N. Rozen and K. Russell. 2004. "Contrastive Focus Reduplication in English (The Salad-Salad Paper)". *Natural Language and Linguistic Theory* 22 (2): 307–57.
Gooden, Shelome A. 2003. "The Phonology and Phonetics of Jamaican Creole Reduplication". PhD diss., Ohio State University.
Kouwenberg, Silvia, and Darlene LaCharité. 2001a. "The Iconic Interpretations of Reduplication: Issues in the Study of Reduplication in Caribbean Creole Languages". *European Journal of English Studies* 5 (1): 59–80.
———. 2001b. "The Mysterious Case of Diminutive Yala-yala". In *Due Respect: Essays on English and English-Related Creoles in the Caribbean*, edited by Pauline Christie, 124–33. Kingston: University of the West Indies Press.
———. 2005. "Less Is More: Evidence from Diminutive Reduplication in Caribbean Creole Languages". In *Studies in Reduplication*, edited by Bernard Hurch, 533–46. Berlin: Mouton de Gruyter.
Marantz, Alex. 1982. "Re Reduplication". *Linguistic Inquiry* 13 (3): 435–82.
McWorther, John. 2005. *Defining Creole*. Oxford: Oxford University Press.
Parkvall, Michael. 2000. *Out of Africa*. London: Battlebridge.
Rickford, John R., ed. 1978. *A Festival of Guyanese Words*. 2nd ed. Georgetown: University of Guyana Press.
Samarin, William. 1971. "Salient and Substantive Pidginisation". In *Pidginisation and Creolisation of Languages*, edited by Dell Hymes, 117–40. London: Cambridge University Press.
Seigel, Jeff. 2008. *The Emergence of Pidgin and Creole Languages*. Oxford: Oxford University Press.
Zuraw, Kie. 2002. "Aggressive Reduplication". *Phonology* 193: 395–435.

Chapter 4

THE FUTURE MARKERS IN URBAN AND RURAL GUYANESE CREOLE

Walter F. Edwards

Introduction

In Edwards (1975, 236–43), I discussed the future markers in Guyanese Creole (GC) and came to the conclusion that Rural Guyanese Creole (RGC) has two interchangeable preverbal future tense markers: *gʌ* (~ gɔ, gə) and *gun* (gʌn, gn) and that an archaic modal form *sa* has all but disappeared. On that analysis, the following invented sentences 1 and 2 spoken by an RGC speaker would carry the identical temporal significance:

1. He **gʌn** buy one when he get money.
2. He **gʌ** buy one when he get money.

In my 1975 discussion, I made no mention of the allomorphs *a gʌ and a gʌn* as encoding future meaning. I did recognize implicitly that the presence of the final alveolar nasal on the future marker was of sociolinguistic significance by pointing out that the *gʌ* allomorph was restricted to the rural areas, whereas the *gʌn* formative was freely used in both rural and urban environments; but I opted to confine my report to the discussion of the *gʌn* variant in urban and rural environments. I made it clear that both *gʌ* and *gʌn* marked the future tense and contrasted the linguistic functions of these two forms with the modal function of *sa* (~ʃ sʌ, sə, si). I asserted (237–38) that "the usage of *go* in Guyanese Creole is identical to the usage of its cognate form *go* in Sranan". In Sranan, *sa* is used with the "irrealis" meaning (Voorhoeve 1957, 382) and "in order to express a wish, an intention or an expectation" (380). In pegging RGC *gʌ* as a future marker rather than a modal, I showed that GC *go* was being used with the same meaning as *go* in Trinidad speech as described by Solomon (1966). Solomon had claimed that "*go* operates as an indicator of future without any distinction between simple and continuous when it is followed by a predictor". My 1975 analysis of RGC *gʌ* had provided independent corroboration of Bickerton's (1974) analysis in which he presented RGC *go* as a future marker and *sa* as a modal. However, in his 1975 seminal book, Bickerton lumped RGC *go* and *sa* together in the irrealis category.

Here, I wish to revisit the issue of whether *gʌ* and *gun* are future markers as well as the related matter of whether or not they should participate, along with indisputable modals, in an irrealis category, as recommended by Bickerton (1975). Then I shall attempt to clarify the linguistic and sociolinguistic contributions of *a gʌ* and *a gʌn*.

The Future/Irrealis Discussion

Winford (1993, 2000) has provided us with the most scholarly and detailed discussions currently available of the issues involved in the future/irrealis debate in Caribbean Creoles. These studies offer rich data and careful analyses—much of what I have to say in this chapter confirms these insights. Winford (1993) argues for a tense reading of Guyanese Creole *go* and Jamaican Creole (JC) *wi*, pointing out that "the dominant sense conveyed by *go* and *wi* is relative 'later time', though both markers always have modal overtones". This decisive position moved the analysis of GC preverbal *go* out of the long shadow of Bickerton's (1975) oft copied, but seldom carefully examined position that GC *go* participates in the irrealis system that includes all modals.[1] Gibson (1982) had been indecisive about the issue, referring to GC *go* as a future tense marker/modal. Rickford (1987) also presented GC preverbal *go* and (preverbal *sa*) as future/irrealis. Scholars who support the proposition that GC *go* marks an irrealis notion are undoubtedly influenced by the fact that the formative can signal prediction rather than certainty. But Winford (1993) points out that "cross-linguistically, most uses of the future seem to involve some element of prediction" and that GC *go* and JC *wi* both express prediction rather than such modalities as conditionality and uncertainty. As Winford (1993) points out, the future marker *go* is used when the speaker believes that the situation will actually occur. This use contrasts with GC *sa*, which usually signals speaker doubtfulness. Thus in sentence 3, the modal *sa* expresses doubt about the future behaviour of the speaker, Mr Bob, who was being urged to vote for a particular candidate. The invented sentence 4 makes a clear prediction about the speaker's future state of knowledge, encoded by future marker *gʌ*.

3. Mi sɛ, wɛl, wɛn di taim kom, awi **sa** noo. (Edwards 1975, 237)
4. Mi sɛ, wɛl, wɛn di taim kom, awi **gʌ** noo. (invented)

Sentences 5–18, all culled from data collected for Edwards (1975), include RGC *gʌ* used as a preverbal maker of future. In all cases, the speakers gave me the impression that they were making a clear prediction based on their state of knowledge at the time. The marker *gʌ* in all cases is most comfortably translated as "will" in Standard Guyanese English.[2]

5. Blackman laka yuself, dey na **gʌ come.**
6. Dey gat rent fu pay, an den dem **gʌ want** sport.
7. Nobady na come, bikaa (because) how dem **gʌ help** yu?
8. When me want am me **gʌ tell** dem se "me want me money today".

Sentences 3 and 5–8 were all uttered by rural residents of Clonbrook or Ann's Grove on the east coast of Guyana, as were sentences 9–13, which include the preverbal collocation *a gʌ*. Standard English (SE) translations of sentences 9–13 are given.

9. Yu put am a sun an i **a gʌ dry.**
   If you put it in the sun, it will dry.
10. Mi **a gʌ reach** up de about nine a'clock.
    I will get up there (at) about nine o'clock.
11. Di down-under people, dem **a gʌ wok** fu eighty dalla dis week and dem **gʌ barra** pun di boss Monday.
    The low-class people, they will/are going to work for eighty dollars this week, and they will borrow from the boss on Monday.
12. When people dead, an if you go **a gʌ bury** dem, an yu pick up da same doti dat cova di grave a buryin-ground an yu bring am, whole night you **gʌ see** di lady or man dat dead.
    When people die, and if you are going to bury them, and you pick up the same earth that covers the grave in the burial ground, and you bring it (home), all night you will see the woman or man who died.
13. Six weeks afta, he a gi flowa; well he **a gʌ** start to gi yu wan-wan side bundle.
    Six weeks afterwards, it usually gives flowers; well, it will start to give you a few side bundles.

Winford (1993, 61) considers that *gʌ* in utterances like 9–13 "is not the future auxiliary *go* but rather the lexical verb *go* inflected for Imperfect". This is certainly a possibility, but I am disinclined to endorse that analysis for two reasons. First, in all cases, the *a gʌ* collocation is pronounced with auxiliary weak stress and not the stress assignments you would expect in a serial verb construction. Second, and perhaps more important, is the fact that *a gʌ* still encodes a prediction that the speaker is committed to, although perhaps less strongly than when *gʌ* is used alone. We can examine this hypothesis by looking at 11 and 12, which include both *gʌ-V* and *a gʌ-V* constructions. A possible reading of 11 is that the speaker is implying that even though a low-class person might earn money one week, the individual will be irresponsible with it and consequently want to borrow money the next week. Thus we have an if-then situation with the *a gʌ* choice recording the condition and the *gʌ* marker signalling the prediction that follows the condition. The same reading is available for 13. In this case, the *a gʌ-V* construction appears in the conditional clause and the *gʌ-V* choice in the main clause: the former construction is hypothetical, the latter recording a prediction if that hypothesis holds. Thus it seems that *a* in *a gʌ-V* constructions is functioning as what Winford (2000, 91) calls epistemic modality. This analysis is consistent with Gibson's (1982) proposal that one of the multiple meanings of RGC verbal *a* is probability. She asserts (1982, 133) that "*a* occurs before verbs as a modal of probability in the basilect". She exemplifies this function with several sentences, one of which follows as 14 along with Gibson's SE translation.

>14. Bikaa mi biliiv hii nak mi, mi **a deed** (Gibson 1982, 134)
> "Because I thought he had hit me, (and) I would probably die"

Gibson further argues that "when *a* functions as a modal of probability the only auxiliary it can co-occur with is future tense/modal *gu*" (134). The modal reading of *a* in *a gʌ-V* predicate configurations proved to be more attractive to me in the end than the progressive aspect reading I first gave it. In that admittedly less controversial analysis, *a* would be a marker of imperfect aspect and *gʌ* would be a main verb in serial construction with the verb on the right edge. That reading pulls *a gʌ-V* structurally and semantically apart from *gʌ-V*, a reading that I find counterintuitive and which does not seem to account for 11 or 13. My sense, too, is that the progressive reading would require *fu* to be inserted before the rightmost verb, at least in some cases.

The Strange Disappearance of Preverbal *sa*

Whereas utterances with *gʌ-V* are very numerous in the data provided in Rickford (1987), examples of *a gʌ-V* are rare. Rickford's full set of data only yielded the following two examples of *a gʌ-V*, presented in 15 and 16.[3]

>15. Evriidee abi **a gu** plee pan da grebe an abi neva see notn. (Rickford 1987, 147, Irene, Cane Walk)
>16. Yuz chro dong yuself a di bangk an yu se "Laad, a wen dis kotlis **a gu kom out** a mi aan?" (Rickford 1987, 163, Granny, Cane Walk)

In the data collected for Edwards (1975), occurrences of the *a gʌ-V* construction were much fewer than instances of *g(n)-V* construction. The relative paucity of *a gʌ-V* is puzzling since it would make sense for a mature grammar such as RGC to want to preserve a construction like *a gʌ-V* that helps to nuance predictions. In considering this conundrum, I was reminded of my puzzlement over what appears to be the almost complete disappearance from modern rural and urban speech of preverbal *sa*, the form that has clear modal implications. In contrast, preverbal *sa* as a modal is a very robust morpheme in Sranan, spoken in neighbouring Surinam, where it participates in a rich system of irrealis markers in this variety.[4] Winford (2000) characterizes preverbal *sa* as carrying a dominant sense of uncertainty about the future and has a number of secondary uses which arise from this, including the expression of possibility, desire or hope for the future. Although preverbal *sa* is heard very rarely now in Guyana and only among older speakers in the rural areas,[5] it is clear that the form was considered to be an integral part of Guyanese speech in the early twentieth century, since written representations of early Guyanese speech use the form frequently. The similarity in the meaning of RGC modal *a* and the Sranan irrealis marker *sa* has led me to speculate that the *a* in *a gʌ-V* is a reduced form of *sa*. That would not be an unusual morphophonemic development because unstressed particles like *sa* (pronounced [sʌ] or [sə]) are notoriously susceptible to phonological reductions. A similar reduction seems to have affected future marker *go* in Sranan, which has been reduced to *o* in many utterances. This line of speculation about the provenance of RGC modal *a* would provide some explanation for the apparent strange demise of *sa*. Following this reasoning would give the following historical process:

Mi sa play ⇒ *Mi go play* ⇒ *Mi sa go play* ⇒ *Mi a go play*[6]

In this hypothesized analysis, early RGC, like Sranan, had two future markers, *sa* and *gʌ*. Later, *sa* yielded to *gʌ* as a future tense, but became available as a modal that collocated with *gʌ* to suggest a softening of the speaker's commitment to the prediction signalled by the tense marker *gʌ*. This *sa* was later phonologically reduced to *a*. Still later, RGC speakers in an effort to reduce the semantic load of the ubiquitous grammatical morpheme *a* began to use other modals, including *mosi* and *coulda*, to encode the meanings associated with *a* when it combines with the future marker *gʌ*.[7] I present this hypothesis very tentatively because I do not have natural or elicited linguistic data to support it and because it conflicts with the Sranan system presented in Winford (2000) where the co-concurrence of *sa* and *go* is strictly prohibited.

Preverbal *gʌn* in Rural and Urban Circumstances

I wish now to turn my attention to RGC *gʌn* by considering examples 17–43.

17. If yu don't want to thief yu na **gʌn thief** . . . but if you want fu thief yu **gʌ thief**.
18. Nobady na bin know one coconut **gʌn value** twenty-five cents in this country now.
19. Dey gat some things fu clean di worm from di pig tongue, because just so de **gʌn stay**, and yu **gʌn find** they feelin sick an they **gʌn dead** out.
20. But a **gʌn** say that still is a bird.

21. Dey **gʌn transfer** you next week.
22. If you **gʌn lie** on me, a just wouldn't stick fu it.
23. A don't know now if a (I) **gʌn like** it, at least when a went then a didn't like it.
24. I understand they gat electric lights and so I don't know what I **gʌn do**.

Example 17, uttered by Kamal, a resident on Mahaica on the east coast of Demerara in Guyana, shows that for this rural speaker, as is the case for most RGC speakers, preverbal *gʌ* and preverbal *gʌn* mean the same, the choice of one over the other being determined by the speaker's often idiosyncratic perceptions of increased formality or informality. In the case of 17, the use of SE *to* as an infinitive marker before the verb "thief" in the first part of the utterance seems to trigger the choice of *gʌn*; whereas the use of Creole *fu* before the same verb later in the sentence elicits the choice of *gʌ*. Whatever the principle that motivates the variation between *gʌn* and *gʌ* in 17, it is clear that the two forms are used interchangeably in this utterance. In example 18, also spoken by Kamal, the choice of *gʌn* seemed to be triggered by the choice of the verb "value", a relatively sophisticated word compared with the synonym "cost".[8]

Examples 19–24 were all uttered by working-class speakers of the Urban Guyanese Creole (UGC) spoken in Georgetown, the capital city of Guyana. In every case, the *gʌn* form is used irrespective of topic or phonological environment. In the scores of interviews done with residents of Georgetown in 1974, not one speaker who was native to the city used *gʌ* or *a gʌ* as the future marker. In every case, the UGC formative had the final alveolar nasal intact. In cases where *gʌn* was reduced, it took the shapes of *gʌn*, *ən* or *gn*, never *gʌ* or *go*. However, the meaning of preverbal *gʌn* seemed to be identical to RGC *gʌ*, namely, prediction of a future event. I wish to claim, therefore, that *gʌn* is the future marker in the UGC dialect. I also wish to assert that it is no accident that the UGC future marker is formally distinct from the RGC markers. I propose that whereas the RGC markers derive from substratal *go*, sharing this provenance with the Sranan cognate, UGC *gʌn* appears to derive from the SE prospective expression *COP-going-to-V*.[9] In no case, however, is the copula for present, in full or reduced form in the UGC expressions. Consequently, sentences like 25 and 26 are unacceptable in UGC.

25. * We are **gən** play.
26. * He's **gən** eat.

Thus UGC has grammaticalized SE *going to* into the *gʌn* marker. This UGC form performs both the straight predictive role of conservative RGC preverbal *gʌ* and the more modally nuanced variant *a gʌ*, the former function being exemplified by 19, 20 and 21 and the latter by 22, 23 and 24. The proposal that UGC *gʌn* derives from SE *going to* is supported by the use of *goin-an*, *gwine-an* and *gine-an* preverbally in many UGC ideolects, including my own. Sentences such as 27–28 are heard frequently in Georgetown and in nonconservative RGC.

27. We **goin-an play** over there. (invented)
28. We **gwine-an see** what happenin over de. (invented)

UGC speakers use *goin-an*, *gwine-an* and *gine-an* in cases where the prospective event is imminent. My proposal that RGC *gʌ* and RGC/UGC *gʌn* derive from different sources seems to be supported by the fact that RGC speakers never use the collocation *a gʌn* as a preverbal future expression, even though I have given it as a theoretical possibility. I also didn't find that combination in Rickford's data.

It is interesting that Michael Aceto (1998, 34) has reported that Bahamian English Creole has the forms *goinan*, *gwainan* and *gwanan* as future tense markers and proposes a superstrate provenance, from SE *going-and*, for these tense markers. He also claims that a superstrate provenance does not contraindicate "a local innovation unrelated to any external factors" (Aceto 1998, 41).

I mention Aceto's article as a means of external support for my proposal in this chapter that UGC dialect future marker *gʌn* modelled on SE *COP-going-to* ignored the Copula unit as being alien to its language prototype and developed forms such as *goin an*, *gwine-an* and *gine-an* to perform specific semantic work within the future paradigm.

Acknowledgements

This is a slightly revised version of a paper presented to the 2004 meeting of the Society for Caribbean Linguistics in Curaçao in August of that year. I wish to thank Madeline "Maddy" Lank, my research intern for part of summer 2011, for her assistance in proofreading this chapter and preparing it to confirm to the stylistic requirements of this publication.

Notes

1. In this, Bickerton followed other Creole scholars who opted for the neatness of an irrealis system over the asymmetry that would have resulted from a tense system for the basilect that included future in addition to +/- anterior. In this regard, Gibson's (1982, 246) tense distinction of [+/ PRESENT] provides an interesting alternative because it accommodates future.
2. I have taken the liberty of using informal modifications to SE orthography in presenting these examples, rather than using the phonemic transcriptions given in Edwards 1975.
3. My reading of 24 is that the *a* is the RGC habitual marker which collocates with such adverbs as *everiidee*. Thus, *gu* in this sentence is the lexical verb.
4. Winford (2000) is a masterful characterization of this irrealis system in Sranan.
5. The single token used as part of the data set of Edwards 1975, given above as 3, was uttered by an octogenarian. Rickford 1987 gives only one token in his recordings of natural speech.

6. Crucial to the validity of this speculation would be whether a native speaker of RGC would accept a sentence like *Mi sa go play* as grammatical and interpret *sa* in this sentence as being identical in meaning to *a* in *Mi a go play*. My own Urban Guyanese Creole competence, which is not offended by the sentence, is unreliable.
7. See Gibson (1982, 127–49) for a discussion of nine different syntactic and semantic function of RGC *a*.
8. In my 1975 study, the variation between *gʌ* and *gʌn* was so considerable in the rural communities I studied that I decided to limit my attention to *gʌn* because it was difficult to control the stylistic variables that prompted the alternation between these forms.
9. See Edwards (1984) for a discussion of the historical circumstance that led to the development of UGC.

References

Aceto, M. 1998. "A New Creole Future Tense Marker Emerges in the Panamanian West Indies". *American Speech* 73 (1): 29–43.

Bickerton, D. 1974. "Creolization, Linguistic Universals, Natural Semantax and the Brain". *University of Hawaii Working Papers in Linguistics* 6 (3): 125–41

———. 1975. *Dynamics of a Creole System*. Cambridge: Cambridge University Press.

Edwards, W. 1975. "Sociolinguistic Behavior in Rural and Urban Circumstance in Guyana". DPhil thesis, University of York.

Gibson, K. 1982. "Tense and Aspect in Guyanese Creole: A Syntactic, Semantic and Pragmatic Analysis". DPhil thesis, University of York.

Rickford, J. 1987. *Dimensions of a Creole Continuum*. Palo Alto: Stanford University Press.

Solomon, D. 1966. "The System of Predication in the Speech of Trinidad: A Quantitative Study of Decreolization". Master's thesis, University of Colombia.

Voorhoeve, J. 1957. "The Verbal System in Sranan". *Lingua* 6: 374–96.

Winford, D. 1993. *Predication in Caribbean English Creoles*. Philadelphia: Johns Benjamins.

———. 2000. "Irrealis in Sranan: Mood and Modality in a Radical Creole". *Journal of Pidgin and Creole Languages* 15 (1): 63–125.

Chapter 5

THE SOCIAL *AND* THE LINGUISTIC IN SOCIOLINGUISTIC VARIATION

Mii en noo (Me ain' know)

John R. Rickford

Introduction

In this chapter, prepared as a tribute to the late linguist and lexicographer Richard Allsopp, I will discuss some of the ways in which sociolinguistic variation in language is jointly influenced by (and influences) the social *and* the linguistic. I will do so by using examples from Guyanese personal pronouns, the area in which Allsopp (1958) made his first foray into quantitative sociolinguistic analysis.[1]

It is necessary to explain at the outset why I need to emphasize the *linguistic* constraints on language variation in the twenty-first century, since the discovery and elucidation of these have been basic to modern linguistics at least since the nineteenth century. Quantitative sociolinguistics developed in the 1950s and 1960s as a way of overcoming the traditional restrictions *against* the use of quantitative data and social factors (Rickford 1979, 27–28), as shown in this striking quotation from Joos (1950, 703): "All phenomena . . . which we find we cannot describe precisely with a finite number of absolute categories we classify as non-linguistic elements of the real world and expel them from linguistic science. Let sociologists and others do what they like with such things . . . they represent that 'continuity' which we refuse to tolerate in our own science [linguistics]." Sociolinguists went on to show that nonlinguistic elements such as speakers' social identity (socioeconomic class, ethnicity, age, gender, urban versus rural background, sexual orientation), style, projected persona and stance (Moore and Podesva 2009, 448) could go a long way to explaining variation in language that was previously dismissed as "free variation". Indeed, as Fischer (1958, 51) first suggested and demonstrated, "free variants" might often be better conceptualized as "socially conditioned variants" or "sociosymbolic variants".

But in our excitement about the social and identity elements in sociolinguistic variation, we sometimes forget the anchoring effect of linguistic structure. This is true, for instance, in the Caribbean-based and deservedly popular model of Le Page and Tabouret-Keller's *Acts of Identity* (1985), according to which speakers' language use is created to resemble those whom they wish to be identified with or distinguished from. As noted in Rickford (2011, 257–58), a minus of this otherwise attractive model is that it neglects internal constraints on variation. In theory, linguistic constraints could be included under the author's fourth rider, according to which speakers' acts of identity are constrained by their "ability to modify their behavior". But in practice they are not, the creators and aficionados of this model focusing almost entirely on the social and psychological factors that might motivate a speaker to use one variant rather than another.

Morphological Variation in Guyanese First-Person Pronouns

Let me give an example of how the social and the linguistic jointly constrain language, from variability in Guyanese personal pronouns. As Allsopp (1958, II.3) noted, English pronouns are terrific for the study of variation and change because they "are the one remaining category of English word for which a fairly full inflection still exists" and in a Creole-speaking context like Guyana offer many opportunities for variability. Personal pronoun variability can be classified as *morphological* if the variation in form represents a grammatical distinction, for example, the choice between *ai* and *mi(i)* as first-person subject markers, where the form of the variant reflects the presence or absence of a case-marking distinction between the subject and accusative/object *mi* or genitive/possessive *mai*. But it can be classified as *phonological* if no grammatical distinction is involved, for example, the choice between diphthongal *ai* and monophthongal *a*, between third-person *hii* and *h*-less *i*, and between tense/long *mii* and short/lax *mi*.[2] As these examples show, phonological variation of this sort usually involves a single segment, deleted or inserted (*hii* versus *ii*), or varying between one phoneme and another (*mi* versus *mii*).

We know from native speaker intuition and observation and from the many studies that have been done on Guyanese pronominal variation over the past five decades (Allsopp 1958; Bickerton 1973; Rickford 1979; Edwards 1983; Sidnell 1999; see table 5.1) that using *mi(i)* as first-person subject pronoun, as in 1a or 1b, is much more characteristic of rural than of urban speakers and of members of the estate and lower working classes than of speakers from higher social groups.[3]

(1a) *mi noo* ("Me know/I know")
(1b) *mi sii di man* ("Me see de man/I saw the man")

We also know that greater use of subject *mi(i)* can reflect a more informal style and that it may be more characteristic of men than women. For Sidnell (1999), at least, drawing on data from a rural East Indian village, the gender disparity derives from the fact that self-referential *ai* "involves not only an assertion of acrolectal competence, . . . but simultaneously a foregrounding of the assumed identity of

Table 5.1. Some social correlates of *mi(i)* as first-person subject pronoun in Guyana

Source	Uses less *mi(i)*	Uses more *mi(i)*
Allsopp 1958 (Georgetown, nonclerical)	Urban .01 (7/614)*	
Edwards 1983, 298 (Georgetown vs. East Coast villages Ann's Grove and Clonbrook)	Urban .004	Rural .44
Rickford 1979, 342–43 (East Coast village, Cane Walk)	Nonestate class .11 (331/3012)*	Estate class .89 (2055/2309)*
Sidnell 1999, 375 (East Coast village, unnamed)	Men .92 (407/442)*	Women .97 (243/251)*

* The measures in each cell represent the relative frequency or percentage use of *mi(i)* instead of *a* or *ai* as first-person subject pronoun. The numbers in parentheses, when available, represent the absolute frequencies on which those relative frequencies are based. For instance ".01 (7/614)" indicates that *mi(i)* was used only 1 per cent of the time, this statistic derived from finding only 7 tokens of *mi(i)* out of 614 total first-person subject pronouns in the data (including *mi(i)*, *uh*, *a(a)* and *ai*).

the speaker" (381) and that "women who use *ai* are more likely than men to be interpreted as self-elevating" (382).

But although the use of subject *mi(i)* by native urban Guyanese is exceedingly rare – less than half of 1 per cent in Edwards (1983, 298) and about 1 per cent in Allsopp (1958, II.19) – there is one linguistic environment in which it is more likely to be found when it does occur: before the negative preverbal marker *en*, as in 2a and 2b:

(2a) *mi(i) en noo* ("Me ain' know/I don't know")
(2b) *mi(i) en sii di man* ("Me ain' see de man/I didn't see the man")

Exactly *why* this should be so is not entirely clear. It may derive from the very common use of *mi(i) en noo* as a fixed idiom (sometimes associated with a joking register or a distancing from personal responsibility), subsequently extended to other sentences with *en* that do not involve the verb "know". But Allsopp's (1958, II:19, 21) Georgetown sample includes several pre-negative examples of subject "me", the last four in this list involving sandhi or reduced forms with the "me" and *en* condensed to a single syllable.[4] The numbers in parentheses after each example refer to the page and line number of the examples in Allsopp's (1958, I:1–181) "Text of Speech Samples":

(3a) *Me e(n) able.* (87/21) ["I am not able"]
(3b) *an' I/me en wan' go back* (102/1) ["I don't want to go back"]
(3c) *But me'n* write (up to now).* (87/18) ["But I haven't written (up to now)"]
(3d) *#Me'n know!* (133/24) ["I don't know"]
(3e) *#Me'n* gat time fo' you business.* (164/21) ["I don't have time for your business/issues"]
(3f) *#Eh, me'n and'stan' wha' 'e seh. Me'n an(d)'stan'.* (168/20) ["Eh, I don't understand what he said. I don't understand"]

The pre-negative favouring of *mi* may also hold in rural areas, before *en* and *na/ no* (with schwa), and among basilectal speakers, although no one, to my knowledge, has yet looked at this. But what this means overall is that although using *mi* instead of *ai* has high social or stylistic meaning, the significance of that meaning (its interpretation as an "act of identity" in the terms of Le Page and Tabouret-Keller [1985]) depends on linguistic conditioning and the structure of variability in the linguistic system – a point that ardent advocates and aficionados of "social meaning" don't always realize or acknowledge. The Georgetown speakers who use subject *mi(i)* before negative *en*, as in 2a, are much *less* likely to do so when the negative preverbal marker is absent, as in 1a *mi noo* or 1b *mi sii di man*.

Moreover, outside the pre-negative slot for first-person subjects, Georgetown and other mesolectal speakers can also use basilectal Creole *mi(i)* as a possessive pronoun instead of English *mai*:

(4) *ii tiif mi buk* ("He thief me book/He stole my book")

Possessive *mi(i)* has many of the same social connotations and associations as subject *mi(i)* – the person who uses it is more likely to be working or estate class, more likely to be rural rather than urban, more likely to be speaking informally, and so on.[5] But in relative terms, possessive *mi(i)* is much more frequent than subject *mi(i)*, especially for Georgetown and other mesolectal speakers. For instance, the Georgetown speakers in Allsopp (1958, II.15, 22, 24, 26) used *mi(i)* rather than *mai* 50 per cent of the time (24/48) – significantly more frequently ($p < .0001$, Fischer's exact two-tailed test) than they used subject *m(i)* (1 per cent of the time, 7/614). This was also true of the nonestate speakers in my rural Cane Walk sample (see

Rickford 1979, 342), who used possessive *mi(i)* 40 per cent of the time (228/569), compared with only 11 per cent of the time (331/3012, p < .0001, Fischer's exact test) for subject *mi(i)*. The generalization also held true for the estate class labourers in that sample, but since their basilectal or Creole usage was already so high, the percentage point difference was smaller: 99 per cent possessive *mi(i)* (498/503) versus 89 per cent (2055/2309) subject *mi(i)*, although the statistical significance was just as strong (p < .0001, Fisher's exact test).

So this is another way in which linguistic categories constrain or influence morphological variation in Guyanese personal pronouns. The set-point for Creole use is lower for the first-person possessive than for the subject category, so *mi(i)* has more potential sociopsychological significance as a Creole form when used as a subject marker than as a possessive. By contrast, we might say that using *mai* has more social force as an English form than using *ai* or that it's more likely to stamp its user as an "English duck". This linguistic conditioning is only visible when one looks outside the variability in the first-person subject slot, looking at all the first-person forms, or even better, at all the singular pronouns or at the entire pronominal system, using quantitative measures or implicational scales. Although the use of Creole versus standard variants certainly has great potential social meaning – regularly communicating information about your social address or background, the persona you're choosing to project or the style you're operating in – its social significance is crucially linked to linguistic structure and conditioning, as Fisher (1958) and Labov (1966) demonstrated half a century ago.

Phonological Variation in Guyanese Personal Pronouns

Continuing to restrict our scope to the first-person pronouns for the moment, note that using *mi(i)* as the object or accusative form has no social meaning in and of itself because there is no morphological or grammatical variation in the first-person *object* pronoun. Presidents and paupers both use "me" as object, there being no alternative pronoun form in this grammatical slot. However, even here, speakers can signal *some* social or stylistic meaning phonologically. For instance, they can vary between the lax, or short, vowel variant (lower classes, more casual style):

(5a) *ii tel mi* ("He tell me/He told me")

and the tense, or long, vowel variant (higher social classes, more careful style):

(5b) *ii tel mii* ("He tell me/He told me")

In my studies (1979, 210–307; 1981) of vowel-laxing in Guyanese personal pronouns more generally, I found that the variants with lax vowel variants (*mi, yu, shi, de* and *wi*) were favoured significantly more often than the variants with tense vowel variants (*mii, yuu, shii, dee* and *wii*) by estate class cane-cutters and weeders

(74 per cent, or 942/1273) than by nonestate class shop owners and white collar workers, and more often by both groups in casual style (71 per cent, or 917/1292) than in careful style (54 per cent, or 792/1467).

But even here one has to be sensitive to linguistic structure because under stress the variation is neutralized, and only the long, tense variant is allowed:

(5c) *iz mii ii tel* (*iz mi ii tel) ("Is me he tell/It's me he told")

Moreover, *mi(i)* is much more likely to be realized in the short, or lax, form (as *mi*) when it occurs as a possessive than when it occurs as a subject pronoun. Our earliest data on this point come, once again, from Allsopp (1958, II:26), who records a vowel-laxing frequency of 91.7 per cent (22/24) for possessive *mi* and a vowel-laxing frequency of 0 per cent (0/7) for subject *mi*. In short, the characteristic first-person possessive pronoun is lax, or short, *mi* and the characteristic first-person subject pronoun is tense, or long, *mii*. My (1979, 210–307; 1981) study shows that this favouring effect of possessive position (usually very unstressed) holds more generally across the pronouns, with a vowel-laxing percentage of 89 per cent (290/326) for possessive pronouns and a much lower vowel-laxing percentage of 59 per cent (1160/1966) for subject forms. (Each of the comparisons/contrasts in this paragraph is significant at $p < .0001$.)

There is one more kind of linguistic conditioning of vowel laxing in Guyanese personal pronouns that is worth mentioning: the proclivity of different pronoun forms to occur with lax variants (*wi, mi, shi, de, yu*). This conditioning is below the consciousness of most native speakers, but it is extremely regular, as evidenced by the fact that Allsopp's (1958) data on this point from Georgetown matched the corresponding data I collected in Cane Walk, a rural community, twenty years later. For instance, here are the relative frequencies of vowel laxing that Allsopp (1958, II) reported (how often the vowel was lax rather than tense, e.g., *shi* versus *shii*) for the pronouns in his study:

(6a) Allsopp's (1958) vowel-laxing hierarchy for Guyanese pronouns (Georgetown): *wi* = .32, *mi* = .56, *shi* = .59, *de* = .67, *yu* = .80

And here are the Goldvarb variable rule factor weights (see Tagliamonte 2006) I found for the lax variants in my study:

(6b) Rickford's (1979; 1981) vowel-laxing hierarchy for Guyanese pronouns (Cane Walk): *wi* = .04, *mi* = .48, *shi* = .68, *de* = .68, *yu* = .84

Although the absolute frequencies differ, the relative ranking of the pronouns in these studies is almost identical (*yu* highest, *de* second-highest, *mi* second-lowest, *wi* lowest), helping to establish that the quantitative data were really capturing a regularity in the language that would otherwise have been unnoticed and for which there must be a linguistic explanation. The explanation I proposed was that vowel laxing, a weakening process, was linked to the relative strength of the consonant preceding the vowel in these CV pronominal forms, as distributed on Hooper's (1973) consonantal strength hierarchy, where 6 is the strongest kind of consonant, and 1 the weakest:

(7) STRONG   6   Voiceless stops

5   Voiced stops & voiceless continuants: *d(e)*, *sh(i)*

4   Voiced continuants

3   Nasals: *m(i)*

2   Liquids

WEAK   1   Glides: *w(i)*

Basically, the stronger the preceding consonant in terms of force of articulation and resistance to phonological weakening processes, the more likely the vowel is to undergo laxing, itself a prelude to vowel reduction and loss.[6]

Summary and Conclusion

In the rich variability of Guyanese personal pronouns, which researchers have mined for more than fifty years, there is much for the sociolinguist to discover and revel in, for the use of one variant over another has the potential of telling us a great deal about a speaker's social class, urbanity, gender, style, acts of identity and other aspects of social meaning, both at the morphological (*mi(i)* versus *ai* and *mi(i)* versus *mai*) and at the phonological (*mii* versus *mi*) levels. But this intriguing variability is also governed by powerful linguistic constraints, for example, by occurrence before pre-negative forms like *en* (favouring *mii* subjects) and by possessive rather than subject positions (favouring lax forms in general). In short, the freedom to enact social meanings is not completely unfettered. It is more like the freedom of "feeling easy in your harness", in the memorable words of poet Robert Frost.[7]

Notes

1. Note that Allsopp (1958) was written in the same year as Fischer (1958), the paper that is often regarded as the starting point for quantitative sociolinguistic analysis, and prior to the paradigm-setting analyses of Labov (1963, 1966). Bickerton (1975, 10) has acknowledged that Allsopp's field methods were generally in advance of his time, but his quantitative, accountable sociolinguistic analyses also were (cf. Bickerton 1973, 641), and they allow us, through comparisons with sociolinguistic data from later decades, to make fruitful assessments of stability and change in real time.
2. So *mi(i)* indicates that the form may be realized as long/tense *mii* or short/lax *mi*.

3. The quantitative differences shown in table 5.1 between the classes in Rickford's study and the gender groups in Sidnell's study are statistically significant, at the level of p = .0001 and p = .0135, respectively, by Fischer's exact two-tailed test. Lacking the absolute numbers on which the relative frequencies in Edwards's study are based, we can't perform the relevant statistical tests on his data, but as the relative frequencies for the urban and rural groups are so far apart and the average number of tokens per speaker is high (83 to 94), his distributions are undoubtedly statistically significant too. Note also that Edward's study includes a nonnative urban group – people from rural areas living and working temporarily in Georgetown – whose use of *mi* as first-person subject pronoun is .27, much higher than the native urban speakers, but lower than the rural speakers who remain in the villages of Ann's Grove and Clonbrook.
4. One should not conclude from this list that all of the seven examples that Allsopp (1958) counts as nominative or subject "me" occur before negative *en*. First, those counts are based only on the first twenty-four samples of speech in his volume I, but for illustrative purposes, he sometimes takes examples (marked with a "#" at the beginning, as in 3d–f, from an additional set of twelve samples that are not used in the absolute or relative pronoun counts. Second, he only gives us five of the seven sentences included in his count of subject "me". Three of those (3a–c) – or 60 per cent – do precede negative *en*, but we do not know what the other sentences are like. Finally, the parenthetical notations at the end of each example refer to the page and line numbers (in volume 1) from which it was drawn, and the asterisks following *me'n** in 3c and 3e mark clear cases of sandhi *miin*.
5. The primary socioeconomic class division in Cane Walk (see Rickford 1979, 120) is between those who work as cane cutters, weeders and other labouring capacities on the nearby sugar estate (estate class) and those who work as foremen or in clerical jobs on the sugar estate or as independent shop owners, skilled tradesmen and clerks elsewhere (both nonlabouring groups are considered non-estate class).
6. To avoid bogging down the main text of this chapter, I will reproduce here the explanation for this regularity that I proposed in Rickford (1981, 205): "The stronger the preceding consonant (in terms of force of articulation and resistance to phonological weakening processes) . . . the more likely the vowel is to undergo laxing. This hypothesis first came to me when I was trying to figure out why the vowel in the pronoun *hii* never underwent laxing (this was also true of *huu* 'who'). The answer seemed to be related to the fact that, of all the personal pronouns, *hii* was the only one subject to consonant loss (the ultimate weakening process): i.e., we get *hii* and *ii*, but no *hi. The extension of the hypothesis to the other personal pronouns is easy once we refer to the consonantal strength hierarchy . . . Leaving aside the case of *ju* [yu] for the moment, note how perfectly the ranking of the pronouns on the consonantal strength hierarchy agrees with their ranking on the vowel laxing hierarchy. For example, *de* and *ʃi* rank equally high on both hierarchies (5-strength, .48 prob.), and *wi* is at the bottom of both (1-strength, .04 prob.) The pronoun *ju* [yu] is an exception, since its initial glide should rank it at the bottom of the vowel laxing hierarchy instead of at the top. But this exception seems to be due primarily to the fact that the semantics of this form are more highly recoverable from the syntactic and discourse context than any other personal pronoun."
7. As Tuten and Zubizarreta (2001, 327) have noted: "To Frost's way of thinking, bonding does not equal bondage. In an interview of 26 March 1954, he defined freedom as 'feeling easy in your harness'."

References

Allsopp, Richard. 1958. "Pronominal Forms in the Dialect of English Used in Georgetown (British Guiana) and Its Environs by Persons Engaged in Non-Clerical Occupations". Vols. I and II. Master's thesis, London University.

Bickerton, Derek. 1973. "On the Nature of a Creole Continuum". *Language* 49: 640–69.

———. 1975. *Dimensions of a Creole System*. Cambridge: Cambridge University Press.

Edwards, Walter F. 1983. "Code Selection and Shifting in Guyana". *Language in Society* 12 (3): 295–311.

Fischer, John L. 1958. "Social Influences on the Choice of a Linguistic Variant". *Word* 14: 47–56. [Reprinted in Dell Hymes, 1964, *Language in Culture and Society: A Reader in Linguistics and Anthropology*, Harper and Row, New York, 483–88.]

Hooper, Joan Bybee. 1973. "Aspects of Natural Generative Phonology". PhD diss., University of California, Los Angeles. Reproduced by the Indiana University Linguistics Club, 1974.

Joos, Martin. 1950. "Description of Language Design". *Journal of the Acoustical Society of America* 22: 701–8.

Labov, William. 1963. "The Social Motivation of a Sound Change". *Word* 19: 273–309.

———. 1966. *The Social Stratification of English in New York City*. Washington, DC: Center for Applied Linguistics.

Le Page, Robert B., and Andrée Tabouret-Keller. 1985. *Acts of Identity: Creole-Based Approaches to Language and Ethnicity*. Cambridge: Cambridge University Press.

Moore, Emma, and Robert Podesva. 2009. "Style, Indexicality, and the Social Meaning of Tag Questions". *Language in Society* 38: 447–85.

Rickford, John R. 1979. "Variation in a Creole Continuum: Quantitative and Implicational Approaches". PhD diss., University of Pennsylvania.

———. 1981. "A Variable Rule for a Creole Continuum". In *Variation Omnibus*, edited by David Sankoff and Henrietta Cedergren, 201–8. Carbondale, IL: Linguistic Research.

———. 2011. "Le Page's Theoretical and Applied Legacy in Sociolinguistics and Creole Studies". In *Variation in the Caribbean*, edited by Lars Hinrichs and Joseph T. Farquharson, 251–71. Amsterdam: John Benjamins.

Sidnell, Jack. 1999. "Gender and Pronominal Variation in an Indo-Guyanese Creole-Speaking community". *Language in Society* 28 (3): 367–99.

Tagliamonte, Sali A. 2006. *Analysing Sociolinguistic Variation*. Cambridge: Cambridge University Press.

Tuten, Nancy Lewis, and John Zubizarreta. 2001. *The Robert Frost Encyclopedia*. Westport, CT: Greenwood Press.

Part 3

Caribbean Lexicography

Chapter 6

THE *DCEU* SETS SAIL FROM BRIDGETOWN ON FRIDAY, 26 APRIL 1996 . . .

John Simpson

In April 1996, I was asked to represent the Oxford University Press at the publication of Richard and Jeannette Allsopp's *Dictionary of Caribbean English Usage* (*DCEU*). The launch event, as it would now be called, took place in the Frank Collymore Hall in Bridgetown, Barbados, on Friday, 26 April 1996, to the accompaniment of speeches by government and university representatives, as well as by Richard, Jeannette and myself.

The text of my speech is reproduced from the next paragraph onwards, not because of any intrinsic merit, but as a starting point from which to observe the influence of the *DCEU*. I have taken the liberty of adding in square brackets some commentary on the subsequent success of the dictionary and on the growth of Caribbean lexicography since 1996. In addition, I have noted some other changes in the world of lexicography since then, with particular reference to the relationship between the *DCEU* and the *Oxford English Dictionary* (*OED*).

The publication of a dictionary which thoroughly describes a variety of English for the first time is an event of both regional and international significance, and such an event happens only rarely. In fact, we are lucky to be experiencing at the moment what may well be looked back on as something of a golden age of lexicography or dictionary-compilation. The *Dictionary of American Regional English* is well under way in the States; Oxford University Press has been fortunate enough to have recently published the *Australian National Dictionary* and will soon be publishing the *Dictionary of South African English on Historical Principles* and a historical dictionary of New Zealand English; in France the monumental *Trésor de la Langue Française* is complete; in America the *Middle English Dictionary* is nearing completion; in Canada the *Dictionary of Old English* is getting well into the alphabet; and in England the comprehensive revision and updating of the *Oxford English Dictionary* is making steady progress.

[The situation has moved on over the fifteen years since the appearance of *DCEU*:

- The fifth and final volume of the *Dictionary of American Regional English* was published in 2012.
- The *Dictionary of South African English* was published in August 1996, with the *Dictionary of New Zealand English* following closely in 1997.
- The *Middle English Dictionary* was completed in 2001 and the *Dictionary of Old English* has published from A to G.
- The *OED* has now revised over a third of the original text.

But perhaps the most important difference between 1996 and 2011 is that many national historical dictionaries are principally available online.]

The achievement of the *Dictionary of Caribbean English Usage* by Richard and Jeannette Allsopp and their colleagues stands alongside these other major lexicographical enterprises and is a credit to them and to the University of the West Indies. The international significance of its publication cannot be overemphasized; Caribbean English will be recognized as a complex and independent member of the list of world Englishes as a result. One aspect of this international significance will be revealed as other dictionary-makers suddenly realize that they have in the past been too complacent. Caribbean facts have been wrong in their dictionaries because there has been no readily available reference work in which they can be verified. Words and senses of words in Caribbean English have been overlooked through ignorance, even though they are often encountered outside the West Indies themselves. The social and cultural integrity of the islands can be examined through their language, and the difference between, say, Jamaican and Barbadian English can at last be analysed from a position of strength.

[One principal result of Richard's work is the introduction of Caribbean lexicography as a regular discipline at the University of the West Indies, Cave Hill campus, with academic programmes leading from third-year undergraduate to PhD. The university now boasts a full Centre for Caribbean Lexicography with one PhD already graduated and on the part-time staff of the centre and one current PhD student, with more expected next year – along with a crop of MA students who are about to graduate in lexicography.]

I can speak with some feeling about the work of a lexicographer: there is so much information to collect, so much analysis to be done, so many willing and sometimes dilatory contributors to cajole. The basic work carries on underground for years before the final publication. In the introduction to his seminal dictionary of slang, the late Eric Partridge wrote in 1937 of "this dictionary, at which I have worked harder than (I hope, but should not swear) I shall ever work again". Earlier in the century, Sir James Murray, the editor of the *OED*, had written to a friend in 1904: "I wonder sometimes whether anybody will ever realize the work that the Dictionary costs . . . but I do not seem to care: I know, and it pleases me, at any practical amount of work, to set at the facts, and force them to yield their secret." Even on publication the concern continues: Dr Johnson knew well enough that "every other author may aspire to praise; the lexicographer can only hope to escape reproach".

But lexicography is also fun, and there is an enormous sense of achievement when the work is complete. I remember once, several years ago, when we were working on the Caribbean term *skank* for the *OED Additions* volume. I had asked the dub poet Benjamin Zephaniah if he would be kind enough to describe skanking to me. He said that he could, but that he would prefer to demonstrate it. As a result, one day he drove over to the dictionary in Oxford and skanked in my office while I sat there – pencil in hand – to document the event. Lexicography is not just a dry book subject!

Reading through the *DCEU* reminded me too that developments in one country may be surprisingly paralleled by developments in another. The *OED* does not contain this use of the noun *borrow*: "You could give me a borrow of your iron" (I've taken the example from the *DCEU*). But the usage is quite normal – if very informal – in British English, comparable to "give me a lend of your iron" and similar colloquial expressions.

National dictionaries are not simply intended to be repositories of "proper" speech. If a term is not just a one-off usage, but is backed up by evidence of continued usage at whatever level of formality, then it qualifies for inclusion. The establishment of such evidence is the reason behind the *OED*'s international reading programme and of the *DCEU*'s painstaking analysis of Caribbean written sources and surveys of speakers of Caribbean English. You will see the *DCEU*'s bibliography contains entries for over a thousand Caribbean sources in its forty pages.

I mentioned earlier that the revision of the *OED* is making steady progress. The first edition of the *OED* was published over forty-four years, from 1884 to 1928. Despite supplements produced in the years following, and a second edition published in 1989 which incorporated these supplements, it has never been revised comprehensively until now. It is an immense work, covering all varieties of English and (potentially) all subject areas from the Middle Ages to the present day. In retrospect it might have been better to start the revision as soon as the first edition was completed. Our files are full of earlier datings for the use of terms, submitted by scholars over the past century: when I left Oxford last week I had just updated the entry for "maypole", including an earlier reference to the term (see figure 6.1) from the early sixteenth century, and revising the definition substantially, as the Victorian editors had glossed it in such a way that the maypole was described as they knew it at the time, oblivious to the simpler maypole, devoid of folksy ribbons, familiar to the sixteenth and seventeenth centuries.

Changes like this are central to the slow and steady work of lexicography and, like Richard's work, result in a more scholarly and accurate analysis of the vocabulary and syntax of a language, and one which appropriately reflects twentieth-century scholarship.

> **2.**
>
> **a.** *Caribbean* (chiefly *Barbados*). Any of various kinds of century plant (genus *Agave*), which are remarkable for their very long, pole-shaped inflorescence.
>
> Thesaurus »
> Categories »
>
> 1750   G. HUGHES *Nat. Hist. Barbados* 223   The May-Pole; *Lat*. Aloe Americana muricata.
>
> 1769   E. BANCROFT *Ess. Nat. Hist. Guiana* 46   The American Aloes Tree, or May-Pole, is ·· usually planted in gardens and walks.
>
> 1848   R. H. SCHOMBURGK *Hist. Barbados* 588   Amaryllidaceæ.—The Amaryllis Plants: Agave americana, *Linn*. May Pole, *Hughes*. The Great American Aloe. *Bois de Mèche*.
>
> 1961   F. G. CASSIDY *Jamaica Talk* II. xvi. 367   A man from Bull Savanna remarked: '*Carito* is the correct name [for the agave], but we call it *maypole*;' and so it is also in the Kingston area.
>
> 1993   S. CARRINGTON *Wild Plants Barbados* 19/2   *Agave barbadensis* Trel. Maypole. ·· Clusters of deep yellow flowers borne on side branches ·· on a fleshy pole-like stalk.
>
> (Hide quotations)

Figure 6.1. This is not the traditional maypole but a Caribbean sense in the *OED*. The label "chiefly Barbados" was suggested by the *DCEU*.

Although the full twenty-volume *OED* is only now undergoing its first major revision at Oxford, the familiar smaller dictionaries – being smaller! – have been constantly revised and kept up to date. The *Shorter*, in its new edition two years ago, is still shorter than the *OED*, but the *Pocket* has expanded so much that it would nowadays only fit into a giant's pocket, and still-smaller dictionaries have crept into the family below it. We are often told that we should rename the *Pocket* (which admittedly even in 1924 when it was first published would have distorted even the largest schoolchild's pocket!). But we have retained the hierarchy: *Shorter*, *Concise*, *Pocket*, *Little* and *Mini*, as they are by now familiar terms. The irony is that the compact disc version of the full *OED* is smaller than all of them. Nowadays people expect so much information in so little space!

The *DCEU* will lead us, I am sure, to expand the size of the *OED*, the *Shorter* and, of course, the *Pocket* still further. It is never too late to assimilate new information. I have already reminded my senior editors that they should not revise a Caribbean entry without consulting Richard Allsopp's work, and the *OED* will be stronger for it. The consistent use in the *DCEU* of the term *Caribbean English* means, I think, that we shall have to replace the rather old-fashioned label "West Indian English" with the now-familiar term *Caribbean English*, and within that broad term we shall be more able to localize usages to particular islands or groups of islands. We already have entries for many modern Caribbean terms: *dread*, *labrish* and *makomè* (either in print or in draft) – because either we have found them well attested in Caribbean sources or in British sources containing Jamaican or other Caribbean speech. But now we shall be able to be more precise in our definitions and descriptions.

[In fact the *OED* chose "Caribbean" as its regional label. There are now 367 instances of this on the *OED* Online database, including such words as *bayberry*, *dutchie*, *facey*, *natty*, and *peeny-wally*.]

I have spoken mainly about the international significance of the *DCEU* as it occurs to me, but its publication is especially the cause for celebration in the Caribbean itself. It doubtless contains many words which you would never have expected to find in a "proper" dictionary; but that simply illustrates the nature of language: it is not always "formal" – modern lexicographers turn over the stones they find on the linguistic beach and report their findings at every level of language, formal, informal, standard, nonstandard, comic and serious. And language reflects culture: we would hardly expect otherwise. I happened to mention at home that there was not as much cricket in the dictionary as I would have expected. I was met with stifled laughter from my wife and elder daughter, who immediately fell to a recitation of Wendy Cope's comic poem "There Isn't Much Cricket in Hamlet", which suggests a view held by many that there are more important things in life! I should say that on closer inspection I found there is more cricket squirrelled away in the pages that I had first thought!

[Caribbean lexicography is on the move – we've already seen the first volume of Jeannette Allsopp's *The Caribbean Multilingual Dictionary of Flora, Fauna and Foods in English, French, French Creole and Spanish* (Kingston: Arawak Publications, 2003), which builds into a steady structure the short "French and Spanish Supplement" which Jeannette contributed to the *DCEU*. Jeannette is currently working on the second volume of the *Caribbean Multilingual Dictionary*, which will deal with Caribbean music, dance, folklore, festivals and religion.

The international community saw yet more movement in this area of lexicography in 2009, with the publication of Lise Winer's *Dictionary of the English/Creole of Trinidad & Tobago: On Historical Principles* (Montreal and London: McGill-Queen's University Press).

Richard's work will also give rise to a school edition, which Jeannette is planning to prepare with her graduate lexicography students, and she hopes to expand this dynasty into other smaller editions – such as a pocket – in due course.]

All that remains for me to say is that Oxford University Press was proud to have been chosen as the publisher of this excellent dictionary and to congratulate the University of the West Indies for supporting this project stoutly, along with the other funding agencies, over its long gestation. I must also offer my own sincere congratulations to Richard and to Jeannette, and to the many other contributors, for producing a comprehensive, elegant and, perhaps more important, very readable work: not a pistarckle, but the father of all Caribbean dictionaries. You will find that it has been worth the wait and that you will benefit in your turn from the international acclaim which the original UWI Caribbean Lexicography Project, now the Centre for Caribbean Lexicography, will undoubtedly receive.

Chapter 7

"COOLIE TYPES"

On the Use of Photo Elicitation in Collecting and Verifying Indic Lexicon in Trinidad and Tobago

Lise Winer

The use of various types of visual representations for getting information, such as photo elicitation – the use of a photograph as a prompt during a research interview – has a long history in the field of anthropology, known most commonly in visual anthropology, though it is used in fields from sociology to advertising (Harper 2002). If one picture is not perhaps worth a thousand words, it is still true that a picture can stimulate memory much more than a verbal description alone (Bravman 1990). Furthermore, "the photo elicitation interview seems like not simply an interview process that elicits *more* information, but rather one that evokes a *different kind* of information" (Harper 2002, 13, emphasis added).

This essay describes and analyses the technique of using historical photographs as found on commercially produced postcards to elicit and specify lexicon; a specific example is described for the domain of traditional Indian jewellery in Trinidad. Some observations on ethical, cultural and epistemological concerns in the particular context are also made. It is hoped that this description will encourage other researchers, particularly lexicographers and ethnographers working in the Caribbean, to make greater use of archival photo elicitations in their research.

Trinidad received a large number of indentured labourers from India between 1845 and 1917. Most of these immigrants spoke Bhojpuri, a language of Bihar closely related to Hindi. The Indic component in both older and modern Indo-Trinidadian – or even non-Indo-Trinidadian – speech is quite apparent, comprising approximately eighteen hundred words.[1]

In the course of fieldwork for the *Dictionary of the English/Creole of Trinidad & Tobago* (*DECTT*) (Winer 2009), many challenges arose with regard to the elicitation, recognition and precise clarification of definitions. This was especially true for vocabulary referring to items that are now archaic or obsolete, not widely known, or very domain-specific. In numerous written citations from the nineteenth and early twentieth centuries, references are made to Indian women's jewellery – very visible, as it was a way of both storing and displaying wealth.[2] However, it is often unclear what the items actually are: "Auction Sale: 1 silver sibundi, 1 gold Julanie, 3 silver coin necklets, 2 silver earrings . . . 1 silver pan hycal, 8 silver armlets" (*Trinidad Guardian*, 15 February 1919). A sublexicon of jewellery words was gleaned from citation materials: words for finger rings, toe rings, anklets, necklaces, bracelets, earrings, nose ornaments and head ornaments. These words had to be checked with people who knew from personal experience the names and connotations of each item.

In trying to find suitable ways to describe or elicit description of jewellery items from local people, a number of problems became quickly apparent:

1. Traditional terms are often Bhojpuri, not standard Hindi, so (modern) Hindi terms are usually not exactly the same as traditional Indo-Trinidadian terms.
2. Traditional items (referents) are often different from modern ones; they may be quite different in design, decoration or material.
3. Resource participants do not always remember the precise meaning of a particular term or do not recall a particular item.

One very useful approach to both eliciting and recognizing vocabulary associated with *gahana* (jewellery) was showing people vintage photographs depicting Indo-Trinidadians wearing various types of clothing and adornments. As others have found, photos "sharpened the informants' memory and reduced the areas of misunderstanding" (Harper 2002, 14). In the case of Trinidad, there is a large corpus of such pictures on postcards, typically titled "An East Indian Woman", "An Indian Belle", or "A Coolie Type"; most of these were published between 1900 and 1930, in black and white or sepia, sometimes hand-tinted.[3] Several of the photo-postcards used in fieldwork are reproduced here as figures 7.1 through 7.9.

Historical Ethnography and Photographs

Photographs, even the most "scientific . . . visual inventories of objects, people and artifacts" nonetheless "represent the subjectivities embodied in framing, exposure and other technical considerations" (Harper 2002, 13), not to mention the choice of subject and setting. As Bravman has described, European photographers have "reinforced and perpetuated stereotypes of Africa and Africans" by the way they "selected, posed and framed images" and "exoticized Africans" (1990, 329). For similar reasons, Brereton has urged Caribbean historians and others to "re-orient the perspective from outsider to insider" and to use photographs and other visual materials to "find windows into past societies and cultures" to "reconstruct a world which has gone" (2005).

Harper considers historical ethnography to be "the memory of community. For photo elicitation to create historical ethnography, photographs must represent the earlier experience of people interviewed. In practical terms, this means that the photos cannot be more than sixty or perhaps seventy years old" (2002, 17). In the case of my research, however, the time depth of the photos was a bit longer, up to about eighty years, that is, only within the slight possibility of someone's living memory. However, although women older than about sixty often recollected the most, some of their knowledge was already co-constructed from what others had told them. In this sense, they were different from Harper's case of showing farmers old pictures of their own community; that is, in his case the "research subjects saw themselves implicitly in images from earlier decades of their lives" (2002, 18), whereas very few of the women I spoke with about the photos had habitually worn much of the types of jewellery depicted in the photos.[4]

In posed pictures, such as the majority of the postcards, it is obvious that the photo subjects knew the photo was being taken – single individuals often in a studio setting. One hopes they were paid something for the use of their image in a commercial context. In nonposed photos, the subjects doubtless knew they were being photographed, though they may not necessarily have been compensated. Subjects are never identified by name, but sometimes are by occupation or social status, for example, "A Coolie Shopkeepers Miss" (figure 7.2). Note that confidentiality, the traditional mantra of the biomedical research model, is obviously not possible with most visual representations, that is, people are not anonymous (Gold 1989, 100). In keeping with general guidelines for *DECTT* citations, potentially embarrassing or critical comments for nonpublic figures are made anonymous. However, people in older photos such as these, with little or no information included, are unlikely to ever be identified, and in most cases, nowadays, that is regretted.

Whether the photographers were local or foreign and what their racial/ethnic identity was in relation to the photos' subjects is at this point unknown. However, it is clear that the photographers thought that some number of people, especially tourists, would be interested in purchasing a copy of the photo. What was their stance vis-à-vis their photographic subjects?

Bravman (1990) notes the problems that arise when, for example, the photographs depict predominantly a controversial or minority group, such as newly converted Christians in Africa. It is certainly worth asking why the Indian women in these postcards were chosen not only as photographic subjects but as postcard topics. Clearly, photographers could not get enough of almost identical photos of exotically, though modestly, dressed Indian women – my own collection has almost forty examples, excluding the obviously poor.

One problem identified by Gold (1989, 101) is that negative stereotyping portrayed in some pictures may reinforce low self-esteem and allow subjects reduced control over their self-presentation. In quite a few of the "East Indian Woman" photos, the image portrayed hardly seems negative on the surface – the women are wearing their best clothing and all their jewellery. However, this may lead to two possible negative reactions from intended viewers. First, a smiling, wealthy, well-dressed woman of the time (e.g., figure 7.3 captioned "Dressed Coolie Woman. All Gold") would have appeared to viewers' (visitors') colonial gaze as exotic, primitive, pagan and sometimes barbaric.[5] Second, the contrast between different sitters in the quality of clothing and quality and number of ornaments is blatantly obvious. The caption "Poor but Happy Coolie Couple" (figure 7.4) underscores this. Some posed pictures are obviously of less wealthy "coolie types", such as a vegetable seller (figure 7.1) nonetheless given the studio portrait treatment, as well as street shots, for example, figure 7.5. It is possible that the photographers desired to depict (rural Indian) life as easier and happier than it was in reality. As Brereton (2005) notes, we must decode as much as possible the literal depiction of subject matter and read and interrogate the illustration, trying to determine both how realistic or how typical are its portrayals and to understand why the artist has chosen to illustrate a topic in that particular way, in that particular setting.

This begs the question of what the total corpus of postcards includes. Although it is premature to do statistical analysis of such collections, I would simply note here that in the actual fieldwork, I used photos not only of women but also of many different kinds of people in a number of different ethnic contexts (e.g., determined by clothing or religious objects) and activities (e.g., agricultural work, specialized métiers, religious observance). This helped, I believe, to normalize topics somewhat and, to some extent, decrease the amount of exoticism inherent in the choice of one subject over another.

Bravman (1990) also notes difficulties he experienced in using pictures in terms of the question of authority. Although a societal outsider and a "Western researcher", he knew quite a bit about the society he was investigating and had been the one to bring back the pictures. Furthermore, his investigation included social tensions, and therefore responses to pictures were often marked by people withholding information they were not comfortable discussing in that situation. My own case was somewhat similar in that I was not local but had some local historical knowledge and, of course, had access to the photos. Unlike Bravman, however, I was not deliberately targeting controversial areas, although I was open to conversations raised by the pictures. In the case of the "Coolie Belles", the most frequent reactions of Indo-Trinidadian women viewing them centred on gender, for example, the difficulties of women's tasks and life at the time and the discomfort and even risk of harm from wearing such ornaments.[6]

Does the historical remove of these pictures alleviate by temporal distance negative portrayals or reactions? None of the people in the photos has thus far been recognized as a relative, and as time passes, this possibility diminishes further.[7] In addition to the straightforward identification of objects, participants' responses to the photos included two potential areas of negative interpretation: social class and personal character (Bravman 1990). In the Trinidad context, the former included comments on the relative wealth or poverty of an individual in a photo and judgements of caste based primarily on facial features and skin tone, for example, "She lookin like a chamar." In a few cases, some viewers considered long, loose, uncovered women's hair (as in figure 7.6) to be evidence of either low caste or questionable virtue.

One photo (ca. 1903–1915), not included here, shows a young Indian woman, smoking a cigarette, standing next to a chair on which is sitting a German sailor in uniform from the SMS *Bremen*. Several people I showed this photo to privately declared that the woman was a *paturiya* (prostitute), and I therefore did not include it in general photo elicitations in this particular exercise, though it would be perfect for future conversations around this topic. Photos of cane cutters working in the fields might once have been a source of embarrassment or shame as low status and poverty of the time, but have now generally become incorporated into the mythic nation-building story of Indo-Trinidad and can be a source of ethnic and familial pride. In general, participants seemed to admire the jewellery and to sympathize with the difficult life depicted in home and work scenes.

An Example of Photo Elicitation at Work

An illustration of the usefulness of photo elicitation – lexicographically and beyond – is now described for bracelets. I must note that although the procedure was highly effective in clarifying and identifying some of these items, I was not able at the time, and have not been able subsequently, to identify all the items depicted in the photos, so there is certainly room for further research.

There are several words for various types of relatively large bracelets, including *baju*, *bira*, *churi*, *churia/churiya* and *mortichoor*. Initial descriptions from written sources and oral reports were usually not very helpful, for example, "a type of arm ornament". However, a great deal more information and commentary was elicited by using the photos. For example, the first distinction made was placement of the bracelet: on the forearm and between the wrist and elbow (e.g., *churi, bira, mortichoor*) as seen in figures 7.2, 7.6, 7.7, 7.8 and 7.3; just above the elbow (e.g., *baju,*) as seen in figures 7.2, 7.6, 7.9, 7.7, 7.8 and 7.3; and higher up the arm (e.g., *baota* and *dhulai*). One *bira* is usually worn at the beginning and one at the end of a series of *churi* or other bracelets in a *churia*, as seen most clearly in figures 7.2, 7.7 and 7.8.

A second distinction was size, more precisely width, and whether the bracelet was composed of one discrete band (*churi*) or several bands placed together (*churia*), as well as shape: a *bira* is made of stiff, heavy metal with knobs on the two ends, an opening between them, as seen in figure 7.1. A third distinction was decorative pattern. For example, despite written descriptions that a *churi* can be stamped, engraved or facetted and the edge may be filigreed, one woman commented firmly that "most churias would be cut into diamaids" (diamonds). A *bira* was most commonly decorated with dots.

In addition to this more "objective" data, women commented on certain aspects of the bracelets that struck them. For example, an item might be considered beautiful, but too risky to show in public: "My mudder well had mohar and thing, dem thief all." Other items were commonly considered uncomfortable or confining: the *mortichoor*, a bracelet consisting of two long solid curved metal pieces with hinges on one side and fasteners on the other; a traditional *bira* that could only be removed by a jeweller. The *churia*, a very long heavy bracelet, was usually worn from the wrist to the elbow; it consists of several separate pieces or two curved pieces fastened with a series of hinges, or little rings through which a wire or pin is put to fasten the pieces tightly around the arm (this is also more accurately termed a *mortichoor*, but is being included as a kind of *churia* because of its placement and size). It is always decorated, often with a raised diamond-cut pattern, sometimes with jewel or stone insets. It is worn in the middle of a series of bracelets. Because each *churi* was quite expensive, they were acquired singly (as in figure 7.1); women often took years to accumulate a "full-hand" *churia*, as seen in figures 7.2, 7.8 and 7.3.

Conclusion

"Photos do not automatically elicit useful interviews . . . [or] evoke deep reflections" (Harper 2002, 20). In order to reach such a point, it is often necessary to "break the frame" of normal views, for example, by using aerial photographs (a different perspective of space) or historical ones (a different perspective of time). The advantage of using black and white or sepia photographs is that they emphasize this latter difference.

Pictorial elicitation can be useful both for general stimulus to commentary or memory and for seeking very specific targeted information, for example, the name of an object. In domains where the referents are now unfamiliar to many people, it may be very useful to include pictures in field research to gain a better understanding, in a more contextualized setting, about various aspects of traditional life by co-constructing meaning with participants about their past and present culture.

This aspect was noted by Richard Allsopp in response to a presentation of an earlier version of this chapter. In mentioning the difficulties he had had, as an Afric-Guyanese man asking about Indic-Guyanese women's material culture, he considered that had he had similar pictures, he might have been able to better bridge the cultural gap he faced. I think this is probably true – not only do pictures present a more easily shared reality, but they enable the interviewer to express questions and responses that are more clearly culturally informed and sympathetic, allowing the development of interactional rapport. A picture is easy to carry, transcends time and space, and just might help elicit and elucidate another thousand words.

Figure 7.1. East Indian woman.

Figure 7.2. Trinidad. A coolie shopkeepers miss.

Figure 7.3. Dressed coolie woman. All gold.

Figure 7.4. Trinidad. A poor but happy coolie couple.

Figure 7.5. Trinidad. Off to market.

Figure 7.6. Indian woman.

Figure 7.7. East Indian, Trinidad, B.W.I.

Figure 7.8. [Untitled].

Figure 7.9. Coolie type, Trinidad, B.W.I.

Acknowledgements

This chapter is based on a presentation titled "Preparation of the *Dictionary of the English/Creole of Trinidad & Tobago*: Selected Problem Areas" given at the Biennial Conference of the Society for Caribbean Linguistics, St Augustine, Trinidad, August 2002.

Notes

1. For a description, history and domain analysis of the Indic lexicon in Trinidad and Tobago English/Creole, see Winer 2005 and 2007.
2. Although not mailed as a postcard (perhaps in an envelope), figure 7.1 is dated on the reverse October 1923, with the note: "Notice the nose ring. A common sight in the streets as well as bracelets around the bare ankles."
3. "The sharper and more isolated the stimulus memory receives, the more it remembers. . . . This is perhaps why black-and-white photography is paradoxically more evocative than colour photography. It stimulates a faster onrush of memories because less has been given, more has been left out" (John Berger 1992, quoted in Harper 2002, 13). Some small details may be lost, however, for example, being able to determine if a necklace is made of gold or silver, not reliably indicated even in tinted photos.
4. Still very familiar, however, is the *sirbandi*, a jewelled headband, commonly worn by dancers and brides.
5. The caption for figure 7.2 has a handwritten note underneath the photo: "I am now boarding with this Lady. I wonder how she kisses her beau. Lovingly, Capitola".
6. For example, a former nurse pointed out that in regard to bracelets "you could put one to four small *churi* together to make one long *churiya*. . . . You had to be careful – it could lead to scarring, or rashes from soap and thing underneath" (interview with Mrs Ena Baksh, 2002).
7. Quite a few such pictures have been included in popular and scholarly books about Trinidad and Tobago history, but as far as I know, none have elicited personal identification.

References

Bravman, Bill. 1990. "Using Old Photographs in Interviews: Some Cautionary Notes about Silences in Fieldwork". *History in Africa* 17: 327–34.

Brereton, Bridget. 2005. "Windows to the Past: A Conversation with Bridget Brereton". In *A Different Imagination*. Documentary Film Series. Produced and directed by Patricia Mohammed (2010). St Augustine, Trinidad: Centre for Gender and Development Studies, University of the West Indies.

Gold, Steven J. 1989. "Ethical Issues in Visual Field Work". In *New Technology in Sociology: Practical Applications in Research and Work*, edited by Grant Blank, James L. McCartney and Edward Brand, 99–112. New Brunswick, NJ: Transaction Publications.

Harper, Douglas. 2002. "Talking about Pictures: A Case for Photo Elicitation". *Visual Studies* 17 (1): 13–26.

Winer, Lise. 2005. "Indic Lexicon in the English/Creole of Trinidad". *New West Indian Guide* 79 (1/2): 7–30.

———. 2007. *Badjohns, Bhaaji & Banknote Blue: Essays on the Social History of Language in Trinidad and Tobago*. St Augustine, Trinidad: University of the West Indies, School of Continuing Studies.

———. 2009. *Dictionary of the English/Creole of Trinidad & Tobago*. Montreal: McGill-Queens University Press.

Chapter 8

CARIBBEAN LEXICOGRAPHY
A Chronicle of the Linguistic and Cultural Identity of One People

Jeannette Allsopp

In compiling this work dedicated to the late Richard Allsopp, pioneering Caribbean lexicographer, linguist, coresearcher, husband and friend, I cannot help but recall the passion Richard displayed as he contemplated the fascinating panorama of territories that go to making up the Caribbean and his own lasting desire to be truly not just of his birth country but of the entire region. These territories are different in many ways, but are truly one in every seriously important characteristic. They are also bound together by what might be considered the demeaning and negative experience of colonization, but out of that, they have forged languages and cultures that are unique and related even across the language barriers set up by the very experience of colonization.

What then is the Caribbean? Is it just an archipelago of islands spread across the Caribbean Sea or is it an entity in itself? Can the Caribbean be considered merely a collection of islands or does this physically and geographically fragmented entity, its territories separated by water, contain within its languages and cultures some quality common to all of them that binds them together linguistically and culturally and therefore causes those that are native to these territories to be easily identifiable as Caribbean? This aspect of Caribbean reality is one of the major features that will be explored in this chapter as the concepts of linguistic and cultural identity are analysed and applied to various aspects of Caribbean languages, lifestyles and culture, thereby showing that the Caribbean is a prime example of unity within diversity.

It is then quite pertinent to signify exactly where the "Caribbean" begins and where it ends, because in this chapter I consider it to be all those territories that extend from Guyana in the south to Belize in the north, including the English-, French-, Spanish- and Dutch-speaking islands, as well as the South and Central American territories that have a sea coast washed by the Caribbean Sea, such as

Venezuela, Colombia, Honduras, Nicaragua, Costa Rica and Panama, Venezuela situated in the northeast and Costa Rica and Panama in the east.

This geographical extension of territories in which can be found a mixture of races, colours, languages and cultures is what we may call the Caribbean, a theatre in which the European nations – the Spanish, the British, the French and the Dutch – acted out their historical rivalries over a period of four centuries. Although the Spanish-speaking South American territories gained their independence in the nineteenth century (Guyana being the exception), there arose a North American neocolonialism with regard to Cuba, Puerto Rico, the Dominican Republic and Haiti, even though Haiti had gained her independence from the French in 1804 at a truly phenomenal cost. In effect, Haiti ended up being under the control of the United States. The English-speaking Caribbean territories only gained their independence in the latter half of the twentieth century, and as for the French-speaking territories, they remain French to this day, as French overseas departments – *départements d'outre-mer* – still in the thrall of France.

However, within this variety of countries and languages, there are many things that bind the territories into one region that is quite different from any other in the world, and that quintessential and elusive quality is what might be referred to as "Caribbean identity".

The question then arises as to how Caribbean identity is to be defined. There are many theories on the concept of identity. One such theory is posited by Peter Roberts in his book *The Roots of Caribbean Identity* (2008, 3), in which he says that there are two basic factors that go to making up identity, namely, the idea of either similarity or difference and the basic, indisputable fact that man is a social being. The idea of similarity presupposes that of difference, which means that those who consider themselves different from their fellow beings are treated differently. It cannot be denied that, because of the human need to communicate with others and to live in communities, people generally tend to associate with those similar to them and to avoid contact with those who, for whatever reason, seem different from them. As a result, social organization leads to conflict, and this fact emphasizes the importance of the concept of similarity versus difference.

The idea of similarity is based on characteristics such as physical appearance, place of birth, general conduct and clearly, language. It is from such concepts that the concept of nation or nationality arises, thereby placing a person as coming from a particular country or belonging to a particular political entity. As a consequence, there is grouping of individuals according to genetic factors, as well as the kind of result that can be seen from the process of European colonization and settlement, namely, a contrastive theory which is defined as a characteristic of Spanish colonialism. See, for example, Adorno (1988, 66–67):

> As a cultural process, the creation of otherness seems to be both demanded by and an inevitable consequence of the subject, whether colonizer or colonized. The

variety of discourse created on – and by – the colonial subject did not stem from the desire to know the other person but from the need for the subject to be hierarchically differentiated from the other person: the colonizer from those whom he tried to subjugate, and on the other hand, the colonized from the invaders who wished to subjugate him. Seen in this light, otherness is a creation that actually allows the establishment and the institutionalization of the limits of identity.

Another factor that should be taken into consideration is the environment, especially the climate, which has a significant influence on groups of people who live together, this specific aspect being termed *ecological determinism*. Elliott (1995, 24) affirms that the environment is a dominating force, which, in the case of North America, fused many different peoples into one: "The North American environment, with its overwhelming abundance of land, created, over time, a new people, distinctly American, whose characteristics succeeded in blurring and, ultimately, in eliminating the diversity of their origins."

In my opinion, it is no different in the Caribbean with regard to the Caribbean personality, because our climate is warm and sunny, and there is the sun, sand and sea. At the same time, because we are separated by the Caribbean Sea, we demonstrate a distinct tendency to insularity, or separatism, that resists the integration and togetherness that should be fostered among us.

Caribbean Linguistic and Cultural Identity

Having said all this, what precisely is Caribbean linguistic and cultural identity? What is it that this concept involves? It has already been pointed out that language is one of the things that separates one people from another and that pinpoints the nationality of the members of a particular group and binds them together as a recognized entity by others.

Linguistic identity can be seen in various aspects of the use of a language by its speakers. For example, Caribbean English, as contrasted with British English, North American English and Australian English, stands out because of phonological differences like pronunciation, accent, intonation and stress. Caribbean English is more rhythmic than the other varieties, and a speaker from any Caribbean English–speaking territory is easily recognized as being from the Caribbean. There is also the question of lexico-semantic differences from the point of view of vocabulary, not only in relation to single lexical items, but also in relation to idiomatic phrases, proverbs and so on. Similarly, Caribbean French can be distinguished from metropolitan French for the same reason, especially in the lexico-semantic domain, which contains a creolized vocabulary, meaning that the Caribbean variety follows the morphosyntactic norms of metropolitan French, but displays combinations totally opposite to those that would be found in the metropolitan variety. Furthermore, Caribbean Spanish shows exactly the same differences, if not in the morphosyntactic domain, certainly in the lexico-semantic domain, through the regionalisms which are manifested in the lexis of the different Spanish-speaking Caribbean territories. Everything that has been observed so far on this theme affirms without doubt the existence of a Caribbean linguistic identity. That fact will be illustrated later on in this chapter when I go into the role of Caribbean lexicography as a faithful reflection of both linguistic and cultural identity.

Given that the language of a people is its culture, Caribbean lexicography faithfully reflects the culture or the essence and lifestyle of the people whose language it chronicles. Williams (1961, 57–70) has singled out three areas within a definition of culture. First, he speaks of the "ideal" according to which culture represents a state or process of human perfection, in relation to specific human, universal and infinite values, so that these values represent a permanent characteristic of the human condition. Second, he refers to the "documentary", or the way in which intellectual and imaginative work produced by the human race is recorded and which contains the best of human thought and human literature in the world, or rather, an area that is very similar to the first. Third, Williams identifies a "social" definition of culture in which the latter is a description of a particular national character, which expresses values not only in art and advanced learning, but also in ordinary institutions and behaviour, or, in other words, the values as reflected in the life and culture of a particular nation, whichever it may be. It is the last area that forms the substance of this chapter and which also includes aspects of the first two, because lexicography in general includes every aspect of the total life of a nation or a people.

Cultural identity is seen in many aspects of the daily life of all Caribbean people, regardless of the existing language barriers between them. It can refer to a great variety of things, for example, flora and fauna, food, festivals, folk religion, folklore, music, dance, and folk medicine, just to mention a few. It is no casual coincidence that throughout the Caribbean, many territories have the same flora and fauna because of a similar ecology, whether this is typically Caribbean (relating to the islands washed by the Caribbean Sea) or continental, meaning the South or Central American continent. It is for this reason that there are corresponding lexical equivalents across the many islands of the Caribbean or across the various countries of South and Central America.

In the area of foods, there exist many similarities between Caribbean dishes, especially those of African, or indigenous, origin. For example, in almost all the territories of the English- and French-speaking Caribbean we find a dish called "cou-cou" in Caribbean English, made with corn flour, okra and butter and prepared in the same way, which is African in origin. In addition, in almost all the territories across the three major official languages of the Caribbean, there is a dish called "cassava-bread" in Caribbean English that exists also in the French Caribbean, called *cassave* in Caribbean French, and *casabe* in Caribbean Spanish, bearing full testimony to the indigenous lexical influence that is so much a part of the cultural heritage of the region.

When we go on to talk about festivals, it is clear that almost all countries have a carnival that is traditionally celebrated before Lent in the territories with a strong Catholic influence, but that carnival also occurs during other periods of the year in a number of countries throughout the region. For example, Barbados and Grenada celebrate their carnival at the beginning of August, Jamaica celebrates it in April and St Vincent in July. In Martinique, it is celebrated during Epiphany and lasts up to the Sunday before Lent. In Puerto Rico, carnival is celebrated from 2 February up to Ash Wednesday, in different forms in the different regions of the country, and in Costa Rica, there are two, the San José Carnival and the Limón Carnival, the latter manifesting many Caribbean characteristics because the people of Limón are descendants of Jamaicans who settled there.

In Cuba, the Santiago Carnival usually begins in the month of June with bands made up of a motley mixture of people in odd bits of costumes, comparable to *ole mas* in Trinidad Carnival. The bands in these festivals are divided into two categories, called "paseos" and "congas". The paseos are distinguishable from the other bands because the music is different. It is orchestral, like that of the paso doble and marches. On the contrary, the conga bands have a mixture of dancers, who dress in accordance with a particular theme and dance to the music of African drums and Cuban musical instruments.

The other three areas that will be dealt with are religion, folklore and folk wisdom. These three domains manifest very powerful retentions of our African past, because all folk religions of the Caribbean are syncretisms of Judeo-Christian and either West African or Indic religions. For example, in Cuba there is santería, which is no more than a syncretism of African gods and Christian and Catholic saints; vodu in Haiti; obeah in many English-speaking territories, such as Guyana, Jamaica and Barbados; *quimbois* in Martinique; *comfa* in Guyana; myalism, Kumina and Convince in Jamaica; and Shango in Trinidad. They all have similar characteristics and similar rites because among them all there exists a very strong belief in the power of the ancestors and a thriving cult of ancestor worship, a belief and practice brought by the millions of African slaves who were forcibly brought across the Atlantic to our region. Ancestor worship gives rise to spirit possession, and dance is a central feature in the various rituals carried out in these religions, as is animal sacrifice.

As for folklore, I have treated this theme extensively in another paper (J. Allsopp 2008). It is well known that there are manifestations of many folkloric entities or characters throughout all the territories of the Caribbean, some of which are entirely familiar, because Caribbean folklore represents the collective knowledge possessed by our people, which stems from similar origins. This collective thought is illustrated in Caribbean short stories and tales, proverbs, customs, beliefs, and superstitions.

The folkloric "character" is not always a person with human characteristics, but can be a particular tree, such as the silk cotton, or a bird or other animal that has been personified to represent a particular phenomenon or phenomena. For example, one folkloric character known very well throughout the Caribbean and even across its language barriers is the "ol' heg" or "ol higue" as it is called in English, or *"soucouyan"*, the name given to it in the French Caribbean. A similar character is "*la bruja*" of the Spanish-speaking Caribbean. In all three cases, the character is represented by an old woman who flies at night, sometimes in the form of a ball of fire, leaving her skin behind and seeking out innocent victims, especially babies, whose blood she sucks before putting on her skin at dawn. Hence the name *soukouyan* in French Creole, meaning "the one who sucks", is found in Dominica, Grenada, Saint Lucia, Trinidad and Tobago as well as in Martinique and Guadeloupe, with variants like *soucouyant* with a silent *t*. Undoubtedly, in many cultural and linguistic aspects, we are the same people.

The third area is that of folk wisdom, which is found in the large body of Caribbean proverbs and idiomatic phrases that abound throughout the region. Richard Allsopp, in the introduction to his publication on Afric-Caribbean proverbs, has made the following point:

> I must concede that I have not found massive, widespread 'African' structural correlation across the some 1,300 Caribbean proverbs of the present survey. Some may wish, on this basis, to challenge my contention that Afric Caribbean proverbs truly derive their conceptualization . . . from Sub-Saharan Africa. My answer to such a challenge is that whereas centuries of common Afric life-experience in the Caribbean would have put a common Caribbean sociological character into maxims which that life produced, their expression could not fail to be underpinned by a basic Sub-Saharan philosophy surviving in a collective memory. (2004, xv)

This is indeed so, given the fact that proverbs all over the world reflect the social history and identity of the people from which they spring.

It is no different in the Caribbean, as a particular example will show. The anglophone Caribbean proverb "one finger can('t) ketch louse/flea/bug" and so on was found in various Creole variants in territories from Guyana across many anglophone islands and Haiti to Belize, to which David et Jardel's *Les Proverbes Créoles de la Martinique* (1969, 101) added about twenty-two correlates in sub-Saharan languages. How do we explain such an occurrence? It could hardly be by mere chance, but rather because of some deep, underlying oneness of folk experience expressed in similar terms because of historical, cultural and linguistic similarities.

Caribbean Lexicography

From all that has been said previously, there is no doubt that there exists a body of material that has been inventoried by Caribbean lexicographers in the Caribbean varieties of all the official languages of the region – European languages, namely, English, Spanish, French, French Creole and Dutch. Such material, which is a chronicle of Caribbean peoples and countries, is the essence of Caribbean lexicography.

Caribbean lexicography, then, is a record of the observations made of daily life, the atmosphere, traditions, superstitions, beliefs, laws, architecture, art, music, dance, folklore, dishes, dress – in effect, everything that happens in the life of Caribbean territories as organized societies.

There are many different Caribbean dictionaries in English, Spanish and French Creole which support the points I have made, and I shall go on to cite some of them here.

Jamaican, Bahamian and Caribbean English and English Creole

Cassidy and Le Page	*Dictionary of Jamaican English* (1967), 2nd ed. (1980)
Holm and Shilling	*Dictionary of Bahamian English* (1982)
Allsopp, R.	*Dictionary of Caribbean English Usage* (1996), paperback ed. (2003); *New Register of Caribbean English Usage* (2010) (posthumous)
Winer	*Dictionary of the English Creole of Trinidad & Tobago* (2009)

Spanish

Agüero Cháves	*Diccionario de costarriqueñismos* (1996)
Tejera	*Diccionario de venezolanismos*, Tomos I y II (1983)

French Creole

Frank	*Kwéyol Dictionary* (2001)
Mondesir and Carrington	*Dictionary of St. Lucian Creole* (1992)

Multilingual

Allsopp, J.	*Caribbean Multilingual Dictionary of Flora, Fauna and Foods in English, French, French Creole and Spanish* (2003)

The dictionaries cited are no more than a representative example, but the following definitions taken from some of them will suffice to show how they chronicle the Caribbean environment.

Dictionary of Jamaican English

- **AVOCADO PEAR** sb; 1657, 1672 avocatas, p1660 advocatas, 1683 aduecades; <Sp (cf *OED*), but somewhat anglicized in the 18th cent by

analogy with *advocate*, lawyer, the meaning of the Sp word; the latter is <Nahuatl *ahuacatl* by popular etymology.
- *OED* 1697. Currently known in Jamaica simply as pear; see also alligator pear. The fruit of the tree *Persea gratissima*; also the tree itself.
- *1657 Book of Continuation 46,* Avocatas, a wholesome pleasant fruit; in season in August. P 1660 *State of Jamaica* (Ms Egerton 2395) fol 489. Advocates, 1672 Blome 25, There are plenty of choice and excellent *Fruits in this Island,* as . . . Avocatas. 1683 *Present State 21,* Supotilla, Aduecades, Star-Apples.

Dictionary of Bahamian English

- **bottle-and-nail** n. a musical instrument: 1978 *A bottle with a corrugated surface scraped by a metal stick, Generally the metal stick was a six-inch nail and the bottle a square Gilbey's gin flask* (Bethel 37).

Diccionario de costarriqueñismos

- **dundo, da** adj. fam. bobo, lelo, mentecato. // 2. Atolondrado, aturdido. // *andar o estar dundos. –as* (referido a personas, animales o cosas). expr. fig. fam. Haber abundancia de ellos. *En esta época* están dundos *los tomates. En los matorrales de aquella región* andan dundas *las serpientes.*

Kwéyol Dictionary

- **manman** (var: **manm, Anman**) N mother. *Kouman manman'w?* How's your mother? (see also: **papa**) ADJ huge, really big, enormous. *Sa sé on manman wòch ki tonbé an chimen-an.* That is a huge rock that fell on the road. (syn: **bidim, matenm**) [<Fr. *maman*] **manman dlo** mermaid. *Jan lontan kwè I ni manman dlo an lanmè-a.* Long ago people thought there were mermaids in the sea.

Caribbean Multilingual Dictionary of Flora, Fauna and Foods

- **pine drink** (*CarA*) (**pine.ap.ple drink**) [paɯn apl drɯŋk]
- *n phr.* A refreshing drink made by immersing pineapple skins, cloves and orange peel in hot water, then leaving the ingredients to soak for 2 to 3 days; the liquid is then strained, sweetened and bottled. **FrCa** *bière d'ananas f.*; **Hait** *goudrine f.* (i) *Le procédé est le même qu'avec les prunes de cythère, seulement pour l'ananas, on utilisera de l'eau non sucrée, la bière d'ananas se sucrant . . . selon les goûts. – DCCT: 125.* **SpCa** *refresco de piña m.*

New Register of Caribbean English Usage

- **rap.so** *n* (*Car A*) A genre of music combining 'rapping' and soca. *And a whole host of ragga soca music which combines reggae, rap and soca in one smooth blend. Keyboards by Junior I.B.O. Joseph and Kenny Phillips on guitar, background vocals by Shades of Black, Major Ranks rapping and Oscar B chanting, and rapso by Barcum. – Cab (Winter 1994/85, p. 12)*
- *[Blend < rap(ping) + so(ca)]*

Dictionary of the English/Creole of Trinidad & Tobago

- **Fishermen's Fete** *n* A celebration in honour of St Peter and St Paul, patron saints of fishermen, held on Sunday, June 29th or the first Sunday afterwards. = St Peter's Day ◊ Its most common form is the chanter-response pattern . . . It is also true of the songs sung on the beach on *Fishermen's Fête*, St Peter's Day, June 29. At that time, each of the beach singers feels that he must make up a song for the visiting fishermen who come from all over the island. (Abrahams 1974, 28)

The entries cited speak for themselves. They reflect various domains of Caribbean life and culture, as they are items of flora, food and music as well as general items.

Conclusion

It is quite clear that Caribbean life and culture are extensively chronicled in the aforementioned works, and they certainly represent the rich mosaic of languages and cultures that fuse to form one Caribbean culture. Unfortunately, space does not permit the inclusion of the immense contribution made by the East Indians who came to the Caribbean as indentured labourers during the Emancipation period and who brought with them new expressions that have been incorporated, particularly in the English of Guyana and Trinidad, into the various areas of everyday life, such as the flora, fauna, foods, clothing, kitchen utensils, festivals and religion. These are fully documented in the *Dictionary of English/Creole of Trinidad & Tobago* (Winer 2009), but the material is copious enough to merit a separate paper or several papers in order to document the Indic contribution.

Nevertheless, after all that has been said about the various Caribbean languages and cultures, Caribbean culture is but a single entity, with national and regional differences between one territory and another. When we look at all the elements that go to making up the culture, the environment, the music, the dance and the food, we are squarely faced with the fact that we are indeed one people who are easily identifiable because of many things, particularly our languages and our music.

To conclude, Caribbean lexicographic works are needed because it is through them and the material which they treat that the Caribbean people in general can be aware of their oneness. Once this is realized, intraregional links can be forged in order for us to survive and face the outer world. One of the best ways to do this is through our culture and our lifestyle, which identify us and lead us to the knowledge of who we really are.

References

Adorno, Rolena. 1988. "El sujeto colonial y la construcción cultural de la alteridad". *Revista de crítica literaria latinoamericana* 28: 55–68.

Agüero Cháves, Arturo. 1991. *Diccionario de costarriqueñismos*. San José, Costa Rica: Editorial de Universidad de Costa Rica.

Allsopp, Jeannette. 1996. *French-Spanish Supplement to the Dictionary of Caribbean English Usage*. Oxford: Oxford University Press.

———. 2003. *Caribbean Multilingual Dictionary of Flora, Fauna and Foods in English, French, French Creole and Spanish*. Kingston: Arawak Publications.

———. 2008. "Caribbean Folkloric Characters as Symbols of Caribbean Cultural Unity". Papers of the 17th Conference of the Society for Caribbean Linguistics, French Guiana.

Allsopp, Richard. 1996. *Dictionary of Caribbean English Usage*. Oxford: Oxford University Press.

———. 2004. *A Book of Afric Caribbean Proverbs*. Kingston: Arawak Publications.

———. 2010. *New Register of Caribbean English Usage*. Kingston: University of the West Indies Press. (Posthumous.)

Cassidy, Frederic G., and Robert B. Le Page. 1980. *Dictionary of Jamaican English*. 2nd ed. Cambridge: Cambridge University Press.

David, B., and J. B. Jardel. 1969. *Les Proverbes Créoles de la Martinique*. Martinique: CERAG.

Elliott, John H. 1995. "Final Reflections: The Old World and the New Revisited". In *America in European Consciousness, 1493–1750*, edited by K. O. Kupperman, 24. Chapel Hill: University of North Carolina Press.

Frank, David, ed. 2001. *Kwéyol Dictionary*. Castries, St Lucia: Ministry of Education, Government of St Lucia.

Holm, John, and Alison Shilling.1982. *Dictionary of Bahamian English*. New York: Lexik House.

Ludwig, Ralph, Danièle Montbrand, Hector Poullet and Sylviane Telchid. 1990. *Dictionnaire Créole Français*. Guadeloupe: Servedit Editions Jasor.

Mondesir, Jones, and Lawrence Carrington, eds. 1992. *Dictionary of St. Lucian Creole*. Berlin: Mouton de Gruyter.

Pichardo, Esteban. 1985. *Diccionario provincial casi razonado de vozes y frases cubanas*. Havana: Editorial de Ciencias Sociales.

Roberts, Peter A. 2008. *The Roots of Caribbean Identity: Language, Race and Ecology*. Cambridge: Cambridge University Press.

Tejera, María Josefina. 1983. *Diccionario de venezolanismos*. 2 tomos. Caracas: Universidad Central de Venezuela.

Williams, Raymond. 1961. *The Long Revolution*. London: Chatto & Windus.

Winer, Lise. 2009. *Dictionary of the English/Creole of Trinidad & Tobago*. Montreal: McGill-Queen's University Press.

Part 4

Caribbean Folklore and Religion

Chapter 9

IN SUPPORT OF AFROGENESIS
A Study of St Lucian French Creole Proverbs

Hazel Simmons-McDonald

This chapter supports a view presented by Allsopp (2000) that Creole proverbs provide proof that West Atlantic Creoles are a family of invented languages that have their origin in West African languages. The chapter uses as its database a small corpus of French Creole proverbs from St Lucia and discusses their similarity to proverbs from other francophone territories in the region as well as to proverbs of African origin. The proverbs are examined from the point of view of semantics, similarity of message and meaning. It is argued that the similarities observed evoke a particular way of knowing and being of a "transplanted" people who, though having redefined and shaped a cultural space in the diaspora, retained the roots of a common cultural heritage in which the use of proverbs was a powerful means of expressing their cultural norms. These similarities, it is argued, are sufficiently compelling to support Allsopp's claim for Afrogenesis.

Introduction

The issue of the origin of Creoles has been one of the most frequently discussed and debated in linguistic circles. Bickerton (1998) suggested that the West Atlantic English lexicon Creoles developed on plantations in the New World, thus making a claim for a strong European source. According to this view, the proverbs commonly used in the region would have developed primarily from the influence of the colonizers in the contact situations that existed on plantations in the West Indies. The contribution of the African slaves themselves is minimized. Allsopp (1976, 2000) presented an opposing view that argued strongly for the African genesis of the West Atlantic Creole varieties. Allsopp (1976) argued that African calquing, a process for which he later (2000) used the term *systemic transfer*, played an important role in the origin and development of New World and other Creoles. His thesis (1976, 2) is that "Africans, first in Africa and later in the New World, interpreted or calqued their native structural patterns in Portuguese or in French or in English or in Dutch – this accounting for the indisputable structural similarities of Papiamentu and English-based and French-based Creoles". Allsopp (2000, 6) pointed to the correlation between African and Caribbean proverbs as "convincing demonstration of genesis". In his 1976 paper, Allsopp presented as examples of supportive evidence ten proverbs from different sub-Saharan African languages, ranging from Senegal to the Congo republics which he had shown to be "near-identical" to and which he had paralleled with one anglophone and four Caribbean French Creole proverbs. He argued (1976, 5) that the proverbs confirmed that "there was an underlying common African way of putting things . . . a 'nuclear African thing' that inspirationally prevailed over enslavement, to express itself still in our day, in our time, on our tongues which have inherited what our forebears had *invented* – new sequences of sounds called Creoles" (emphasis in original).

Aub-Buscher (1989, 2), as well as others, cautioned that adequate descriptions of the vocabulary of African languages were necessary for the task of determining lexical sources. Although etymological investigation – that is, relating to lexical remnants and development of word meaning – is perhaps the ultimate area for proving genesis, the lack of descriptions and texts with examples of African proverbs in their original languages makes this aspect of the work challenging. Some of that work has been undertaken by some authors, for example, Warner-Lewis (1991, 84, 109) in Trinidad. Quite apart from etymological considerations, there are striking similarities in the French Creole proverbs in different francophone territories within the region as well as varieties in the Pacific Rim and Louisiana in the United States. An examination of the available corpus also points up other areas that provide strong evidence of a common source for French Creole proverbs. These include sameness of meaning, similarities in form, use of metaphor, context of use, theme and content. Robertson (2004) also points to the use of symbolism in the proverbs that "derives from the fact that the proverbs are themselves part of a wider range of understandings and behaviours that impact directly on attempts to educate the Caribbean citizen, in both formal and informal structures. The proverb represents all those aspects of Caribbean experience which have the potential to enhance the capacity to analyse, evaluate and inform" (5).

We are all aware that proverbs are not unique to the francophone territories in the Caribbean. As Allsopp (2000, xxi) pointed out, "Proverbs are the orature of the folk: all folk, everywhere, through all recorded time. And they are therefore bound to embody mountains of human experience and wisdom. . . . The study of a people's proverbs is the study of what undergirds, frames and shapes that people's life-ways, even when those people have themselves forgotten or are inclined to forget their hidden roots, or fail to recognize the spread of their own branches." It is the forgetting of the hidden roots that results in historical reconstructions that may not represent the reality of the historical situation and its influence on the present. Although it is true, as Robertson says, that Caribbean proverbs "encapsulate hundreds of years of experience of colonialism, plantation slavery and indentureship and the lessons learnt from through the centuries" (2004, 5), it is also true that the similarities in the proverbs reveal a common heritage which is rooted in a common life experience further afield than those born on plantations in far-flung territories in the New World through contact between disparate colonizing groups and slaves.

Similarities in content, theme, characters, message and meaning were evident in the examples from the collections of Caribbean proverbs that I examined. In the preface to the David and Jardel (1969) collection of French Creole proverbs, Gilbert Gratiant comments on the similarities between characters in the French Creole proverbs and those of African folklore. He says,

> Les proverbs antillais sont bien un reflet de la vie antillaise: la division sociale en Blancs, Noirs et Mulâtres s'y retrouve. Les animaux familiers: chien, chat, rat, bœuf, cheval, s'y retrouve . . . Mais on retrouve aussi les personages du folklore africain: l'éléphant, le tigre . . . qui n'existent pas aux îles, et enfin compère Lapin qui, par sa ruse et son esprit, correspond au Renard de la fable française. (2–3)[1]

Allsopp (2004) also found striking duplicates among proverbs in English lexicon Creoles. He noted that when these showed up in territories distant from each other,

> the question of natural diffusion – without substantial inter-territorial transfer of slaves, which (except in very few cases such as Guyana and Barbados, Barbados and Jamaica) did not happen – was not a reasonable supposition. When a proverb like **Man chat / talk too much (h)e pay (h)e fadda debt** . . . turns up 5 times, either on hand-written cards or in printed collections (though with slight variations) in Antigua, Guyana, Jamaica and the US Virgin Islands, one must seek an explanation, if only prompted by the sheer oddity of the maxim. Finding none (as I didn't in that case) still left the suspicion that there could be some common Afro-ancestral source. (xvii)

The Corpus

The examples presented here come from four territories in the eastern Caribbean region: the French island of Guadeloupe – exemplifying one strand – Haiti, Dominica and St Lucia. I began with St Lucian proverbs and then examined other sources to find identical or similar French Creole proverbs.[2] Allsopp's definition provided a yardstick for those expressions that could be considered proverbs. He defined a proverb as "a gem of utterance sparkling with a message that a hearer would like to remember in that form" (2004, xvi). He also suggested three characteristics of proverbs, namely, that they are stored and used by all human cultures on Earth; that they are "general statements" that carry a "message that is usually short, often witty and always easy to remember"; and that they "offer a guide (simple or difficult, sometimes questionable) in solving everyday human problems" (xvi). The examples presented here exhibit these characteristics, for the most part. Examples considered to be wise sayings but which did not seem to embody the last two characteristics mentioned were not included for discussion.

The thematic content of the proverbs ranges across all aspects of life. They reflect on family life; on society and social issues; on animal behaviours, sometimes using these as a basis for commentary on human strengths and failings; on codes of conduct; and on the environment. Some are philosophical reflections on life in general. The St Lucian examples seemed to fall naturally into several of these categories. However, a few samples for three categories are presented in this chapter: (i) family and relationships, (ii) animals and their behaviour, and (iii) philosophical observations about different subjects. The tables that follow group the examples according to these categories. There is some measure of overlap because some proverbs could be included in more than one category on the basis of the message. For example, proverbs relating to such categories as flora, fauna and even animal behaviour often carry messages that relate to other areas, such as belief systems, behavioural norms and religion.

The St Lucian French Creole proverbs (SLFCP) are presented in the first column because they were the starting point of the investigation and provided the core from which the selection was made. Correlates from Dominica (DFCP), Guadeloupe (GFCP) and Haiti (HFCP) are presented in the second, third and fourth columns, respectively. The fifth column indicates the African country/countries where these proverbs have so far been attested. The sixth column gives the language of the groups that use them, and the final column gives a literal and/or general meaning of the proverb. An X in a column indicates that no corresponding information was found (in the particular country) for the St Lucian examples listed, but an attempt was made in this chapter to include only those examples for which African correlates were found. The original St Lucian corpus that I consulted totalled approximately 150. Of these, only a small set for each of the three categories is listed in this presentation. Ongoing work involves closer examination of the existing corpus and procuring other sources of proverbs that have been identified but were not available for consultation in the preparation of this chapter. The orthography developed by the subcommittee of the Orthography Workshop in St Lucia is used to represent the St Lucian and, in some instances, the Dominican varieties.[3]

It must be noted that in the corpus examined, there were several entries that had sources other than African sources. Some of these were of European origin and could well have emerged in the contact situations in the territories. In the category reflecting family life and relationships, for example, a subset of the corpus examined indicated a larger number of correlates with African sources than with French sources. Only a small number were listed as St Lucian without having any other source, and one might assume that those for which a source cannot be identified may have emerged exclusively within the St Lucian context of slavery and colonialism. Of the fifteen examples examined, eight had African correlates, France was identified as a source for three, and two were listed as exclusively St Lucian. This is mentioned merely as an additional instance that could conceivably be used to argue the case for Afrogenesis. If of the samples listed in the corpus the larger number of St Lucian proverbs have African correlates compared with those with France or St Lucia as origins, this would provide further evidence for the Afrogenesis hypothesis.

The David and Jardel (1969) collection provided useful information on common sources of some proverbs. However, in the case of the African correlates, the proverbs are given in French and not in the African source language. This limitation precluded the possibility of examining the corpus for African lexical correlates. As Aub-Buscher (1989) noted, without the availability of adequate descriptions of the relevant African languages, attribution of a lexical item to a particular "locality" (African source) is difficult. Nevertheless, the David and Jardel text does indicate countries in which identical proverbs occur, so it was possible to identify a common African source for the proverbs listed.

Discussion of Sample

The seven examples listed in table 9.1 (family life and relationships) all have correlates in the African languages/groups listed in column 6. If we examine the first four proverbs in table 9.1 in terms of meaning and message, it is clear that their meanings are similar to the renderings from these African versions, given in French:

1. *Lorsque les yeux pleurent, le nez ne reste pas non plus tranquille.* (Liberia – Kru)
   Quand L'œil pleure, le nez est humide. (Cameroun – Duala)
   Quand les yeux pleurent, le nez pleure. (Gabon – Mpongoué)
   Quand lœil pleure, le nez coule. (Congo-Kinshasa – Mongo)
2. *Question de commerce il n'y a pas de lien de famille.* (Togo – Moba, Gurma)
   En ce qui concerne L'argent il n'y a pas de lien de famille. (Angola – Umbundu)
3. *Les dents et les gencives se batten.* (Mali – Minyanka)
   Les dents et la langue se querellent. (Côte d'Ivoire – Baoulé)
4. *"Si javais su" est toujours superflu.* (Guinea – Mandingo)
   "Si javais su" n'est jamais avant, mais toujours en retard. (Mali – Minyanka)

The first proverb uses the body parts of the eyes and the nose to point to a message of close relationship. Indeed, both first and the third proverbs use similar means to convey somewhat different messages. The interpretation of the messages of these proverbs is the same in the African and Antillean renderings. The use of similar metaphors (eyes/nose; teeth/gums/tongue) to convey messages of closeness suggests some common perceptions and understandings about human relationships. The fifth proverb in table 9.1 has a single source indication, Upper Volta. In it we can get the following rendering in French: *La vache n'est jamais fatiguée de porter ses mamelles* [Mossi]. This African example

Table 9.1. Proverbs having to do with family life and relationships

SLFCP	DFCP	GFCP	HFCP	African correlates/sources	Language/tribal group	Translation/meaning
1. Zyé pléwé, né koulé dlo.	Sa ki fè zyé, fè né.	Piqué nez, ziés ka pléré, couri dleau.	Nien prend coup, gés	Liberia, Nigeria, Congo-Kinshasa	Kru, Hausa, Mongo	Literal: The eyes cry and the nose runs.
2. Koté lagent	X	X	Coté lintéret pa ni fami.[4]	Togo, Angola pas gain fami.	Moba, Gurma, Umbundu	Don't mix business and family matters.
3. Dan avek lanng toujou gagnyé kont.	Dans ek lang ka fè twen.	Dents et langue ka fâché.	Dents mode langue.	Mali, Ghana, Côte d'Ivoire	Minyanka, Bambara, Gonja, Baoulé	Literal: Teeth and tongue are always at odds. Close associations can breed dissent.
4. (a) Avan mayé sé chè doudou, apwé sé si mwen té sav. (b) 'Si mwen té sav' toujou dèyè.	(a) Lè lanmou sé chè kòkòt lè ou mayé sé chou manman'w. (b) 'Si mwen té sav' toujou twòp ta.	X	'Si m'té connin' toujou déié.	Guinea, Mali, Togo, Dahomey, Nigeria, Cameroun	Mandingo, Minyanka, Moba, Gurma, Fon, Bafut, Bassa	(a) Literal: Before it's "Dear sweetheart"; after, it's "If I had known". (b) "If I had known" is always after(wards). Hindsight is 20-20 vision.

5. Tété pa janmen twò lou pou lèstomak.	Tété pa janmen twò lou pou lèstomak.	Tétées pas janmain trop loud pou lestomaque.	Upper Volta	Mossi	Literal: Breasts are never too heavy for the stomach. The problems of a loved one are never too burdensome to bear.[5]
6. Faute manman ou tété kabwite.	Faute manman ou ka tété magranne.	Là ou pé pas tété manman ou ka tété cabrite.	Mali, Senegal	Peul, Bambara, Malinké, Wolof, Sérèr	Literal: If baby can't be nursed by mother, he'll be nursed by a goat.
7. Ou ka fè yche, ou pa ka fè tchè yche.	Manman ka fè zanfans, mé pa ka fè tchè yc.	Ou ka fait zenfants, ou pas ka fait coeù io.	X	Congo	Kongo	Literal: One makes children, one doesn't make the child's heart. A parent cannot determine (be held responsible for) a child's disposition or personality.

(as expressed in French) perhaps better conveys the intended message: "God never gives one more problems than one can bear" or "The burdens of a loved one are never too burdensome to bear."

The use of *kabwite* in the St Lucian example of the sixth proverb is odd. In the Dominica and Haiti examples, the words used are for "grandmother". Interestingly, in the English lexicon of the Guyana example, the meaning of "grandmother" is also indicated. The meaning of this proverb in these varieties is "If baby can't get mamma, he suck granny", which is a more gentle expression. In all the African examples – three from different languages in Mali (Peul, Bambara and Malinké), and in the example from Senegal, which also has two languages listed (Wolof, Sérèr), the word *grandmother* is used. The differences between the St Lucian and Guadaloupean renderings may have gone through some change or corruption.

The category of proverbs dealing with animals and animal behaviour (see table 9.2) had the most examples. Here again, we see commonality in the use of animal names. It will be noted that the Caribbean examples reference the cat, but the African examples reference the tiger. This is expected where the environment and way of life in the New World did not have the same types of large animals as in Africa. However, the French Creole proverbs preserve the tiger image through reference to the cat, which is from the same family and ostensibly has some similar characteristics. An examination of the examples from both parts of the world shows a consistency in the substitutes used in the French Creole proverbs. Where a large feline creature occurs in the African example, an animal from a corresponding subset of the same genus is used in the Caribbean examples. Hence, for the most part, one finds a preservation of meaning and message but a recasting, incorporating the creatures and images within the new environment.

There were no African correlates found in the case of the first and second examples. A French source is given for the first proverb, and the second proverb does not have a source, which might suggest that it emerged within the Caribbean. The only source listed for the fourth proverb is Ghana. In French, the rendering *Deux crocodiles ne vivent pas dan un même trou* uses crocodiles instead of *kwab* (crabs). Yet note the St Lucian example selects an animal that more readily fits the image and message being conveyed.

The category of proverbs involving philosophical observations about life in general (see table 9.3) contained many more attestations from African varieties than the other two categories. Corresponding examples were found for selected varieties in the Pacific Rim as well, which makes the notion of emergence in a transplanted location a little more difficult to accept. It is more likely that the proverbs originated in Africa and were transplanted with the peoples who used them. They would have gone through some minor changes with regard to use of specific images (as in the case of crabs for crocodiles and cat for tiger) that would have corresponded to the differences between the two environments. Yet the differences in the St Lucian examples retained as close a correspondence as possible with the original image and retained the essential message of the proverbs. Thus far, the weight of evidence in the entries in several of the sources examined provides a reasonably convincing picture for common African sources.

Table 9.2. Proverbs involving animals and animal behaviour

SLFCP	DFCP	GFCP	HFCP	African correlates/sources	Translation/meaning
1. Chyen pa ka fè chat.	X	Chyen pa'a fè chat.	Chyen pa'a fè chat.	X	Dogs do not make (give birth to) cats.
2. Ti chyen ni fòs douvan kay mèt-li.	X	Ti chyen ni fòs douvan kay mèt-li.	Chyen gen fòs douvan kaz mèt-li.	X	One is strong on one's own turf. A man is king in his home.
3. Bay nèg pyé I ka pwan lanmenn.	Bay nèg pyé I ka pwan lanmenn.	Ba io pied, io ka prend main.	X	Central Africa (Banda)	Give a person an inch and s/he'll take a mile.
4. Dé mal-kwab pa ka wété an menm twou.	Dé mal-kwab pa ka wété andan an twou.	Pa ni dé mal-crabes adans an même trou.	Dé taureau pas commandé nnen meinme savanne.	Ghana	Two male crabs won't live in the same hole.
5. Wavèt pa ni wézon douvan poul.	Wavèt pa janmen ni wézon douvan poul.	(a) Poul pa jen ni rézon douvan. manglous (b) Ravet pa gen ni rézon douvan poul.	Ravet pa jen ni rézon douvan poul.	Togo (Moba, Gurma)	The cockroach never has any rights in the presence of the fowl.

Table 9.2. Proverbs involving animals and animal behaviour (continued)

SLFCP	DFCP	GFCP	HFCP	African correlates/sources	Translation/meaning
6. Chat pa la, wat ka bay bal.	Chat pa la, wat ka bay bal.	Chat pa la rat ka bay la.	Lè chat pa la, rat bay kalinda.	Guinea, Togo (Moba, Gurma), Dahomey, Mali, Haute-Volta, Congo	When the cat's away, the rats (mice) will play (have a ball).
7. Bèf pa jamen di savann mèsi.	Bèf pa jamen di mèsi savann.	Bèf pa ka amen di savann mèsi.	Bèf pa jamn rèmésyé savann.	Haute-Volta (Gourmanche)	Literal: The cow never thanks the field (pasture). Ungrateful people never remember their benefactors.
8. Zafè kabwit pas zafè mouton.	Zafè kabwit pas zafè mouton.	Zaffai à cabrite cé pas zaffai à mouton	Zaffai mouton pas zaffai cabrite	Zaïre (Baluba) Togo (Ewé)	The business of others should not concern you.
9. Avan zaboka té bay makak té ka nouwi yche-li.	X	Avant rrangousse té vini, zagouti té ka viwe	Avant maï vète té dom-mein macaque té mange graomne-bois	Haute-Volta (Gourounsi) Togo	No one is indispensable.
10. Sé bon tchè kwab ki fè'y pa ni tèt.	Sé bon tchè kwab ki fè l pa ni tèt.	X	Cé bon coeü crabe qui fait le sans tête.	Ghana (Nzema), Togo (Moba, Gurma)	An individual is the victim of his/her own emotions/feelings.

Table 9.3. Proverbs that involve philosophical observations about life in general

SLFCP	DFCP	GFCP	HFCP	African correlates/sources	Translation/meaning
1. (a) Avan mayé sé "Shè, doudou"; apwé sé "Si mwen té sav". (b) Si mwen té sav "toujou dèyè.[6]	(a) Lè lanmou sé "shè kokot / (cocote). Lè ou mayé sé "tchou manman'w". (b) "Si mwen té sav" toujou twò ta.	X	"Si m'té connin" toujou déiè.	Guinea (Mandingo), Mali (Minyanka), Togo (Moba, Gurma), Haute-Volta (Mossi, Gourmanche), Dahomey (Fon), Nigeria (Bafut), Cameroun (Bassa)	Hindsight is 20-20 vision.
2. Kodonyé toujou pli mal chaussé.	Kodonyé toujou mal chaussé.	X	X	Togo (Moba, Gurma)	You do certain things for others but neglect to do them for your own.
3. Yon sèl dwèt pa sa pwan pis.	Yon sèl dwèt pa sa.	X	Gnou douète pas ka, tué pou.	Zaïre (Mongo, Bwaka, Kikaya),[7] Senegal (Wolof), Guinea (Soussou), Ghana (Ashanti), Haute-Volta (Gourmanche), Togo (Ouatchi), South Dahomey, Nigeria (Oron/Bafut),[8] Cameroun (Ewondo, Bassa, Boulou, Mézimé), Gabon (Ambèdè), Central Africa	Literal: One finger alone can't catch fleas.

Acknowledgements

I am grateful to Professor Richard Allsopp and Dame Pearlette Louisy who provided me with some rare collections of proverbs. This chapter is a revised version of a paper presented at the St Lucia Studies Conference 2004, on the thirtieth anniversary of the Folk Research Centre there.

Notes

1. An approximate translation: The Antillean proverbs reflect the way of life in the Antilles, the social divisions of whites, blacks and mulatto are found in them. The familiar animals: the dog, cat, rat, cow, horse are found there . . . But one also finds the characters of African folklore: the elephant, the tiger . . . which do not exist in the islands, and therefore one finds Mr Rabbit who, through his cunning and spirit, corresponds to the fox of the French fable.
2. See, for example, a small collection by Lister Simmons (1955), *Some Creole Proverbs of St. Lucia*. Other examples can be found in Fontaine and Weekes (1994), *Kwéyòl: A Basic Guide*.
3. See Louisy and Turmel-John (1983).
4. This is also attested in Mauritius in the Pacific: *Larzent napas éna famille*.
5. This has several interpretations – it is also related to religious belief, namely, that God never gives one more burdens than one can bear.
6. Examples for this were also found in examples from Louisiana and Cuba.
7. There are slightly different renderings in these varieties: *Un seul doigt ne suffit pas pour enlever un pou de la tête* (Mongo); *Un suel doigt ne prend pas de fourmis rousse* (Bwaka); *Un deul doigt ne décortique pas l'arachide* (Kikaya).
8. There are two renderings in these languages in Nigeria: *Un seul doigt n'enlève pas do pou* (Oron) and *Une main ne peut pas attacher de paquet* (Bafut).

References

Agence de Coopération Culturelle et Technique. 1987. *1000 Proverbes Créoles de la Caraïbe Francophone*. Paris: Author.

Allsopp, Richard. 1976. "The Case for Afrogenesis". Paper presented at the Conference of the Society for Caribbean Linguistics, Guyana, August 1976.

———. 2000. "The Afrogenesis of Caribbean Creole Proverbs". Paper presented at the Conference of the Society for Caribbean Linguistics, Mona, Jamaica, August 2000.

———. 2004. *A Book of Afric Caribbean Proverbs*. Kingston: Arawak Publications.

Aub-Buscher, Gertrud. 1989. "African Survivals in the Lexicon of Trinidad French-Based Creole". *Occasional Paper* 23. The University of the West Indies, Jamaica, Trinidad, Barbados.

Bickerton, Derek. 1998. "A Sociohistoric Examination of Afrogenesis". *Journal of Pidgin and Creole Linguistics* 13 (1): 63–92.

Crowley, Daniel, and Lister Simmons. 1955. *Some Creole Proverbs of St.Lucia*. Castries, St Lucia: The Voice Printery.

David, Bernard, and Jean-Pierre Jardel. 1969. *Les Proverbes Créoles de la Martinique: Langage et Société*. CERAG.

Fontaine, Marcel, and Allan Weekes. 1994. *Kwéyòl: A Basic Guide*. St Lucia: Folk Research Centre.

Louisy, Pearlette, and Paule Turmel-John. 1983. *A Handbook for Writing Creole*. Special Issue No. 1. Castries, St Lucia: Research St Lucia Publications.

Robertson, Ian. 2004. "The Role of Proverbs in Developing Critical Thinking Skills in the Caribbean Child". Paper presented at the Critical Thinking Symposium, University of the West Indies, St Augustine, 15 January 2004.

Warner-Lewis, Maureen. 1991. *Guinea's Other Suns: The African Dynamic in Trinidad Culture*. Dover, MA: The Majority Press.

Chapter 10

MINGI MAMMA

Continuities and Metamorphoses in a Colonial Context

Ian E. Robertson

In 1627, a party of twenty-six, led by the Dutch merchant Abraham van Peere, set out from Vlissingen to establish what was to become the private colony of Berbice. It was to be a private colony for much of its subsequent history. The fact that Berbice was under the patronage of the Vlissingen merchant Abraham van Peer might well be responsible for the significant unavailability of documents that could ensure a positive statement on the demographic and other sociohistorical matters related to the early development of the colony. Between its founding in 1627 and the visit of Adrian van Berkel in 1670, there is virtually no documentation of the early development of the colony. The sole exception is perhaps Adam Jones's (1988) indication that at least one 1682 Prussian record indicates that a cargo of about five hundred slaves from Calabar was to have been transported to the colony. The information is significant if only because it provides what could be the most significant explanation for a linguistic phenomenon of which the word *mingi* is representative.

According to Jones, "the other ship, whose cargo included <a large kettle, 50 lbs tobacco, a drum, and two hundred [pairs of] shackles> was to transport the remaining 500 slaves to the colony of the Zeeland family van Peer on the Berbice river in what is now Guyana" (285) (<arrows> in original). In the absence of actual historical documents, the source of significant linguistic input become crucial since the presence of linguistic evidence could be accounted for only by the existence of significant influence from that particular source.

In the case of Berbice, this linguistic input has been demonstrated to have come from the Eastern Ijo cluster of languages of the Niger Delta area (Smith, Robertson and Williamson 1987).

The single most significant indication of the nature of the West African presence in the Berbice colony is the evidence of seminal linguistic input into the

Creole language that has come to be known as Berbice Dutch. This language, which was both the main means of intragroup communication and the main language of the slaves and their descendants in the Berbice colony, is known to possess the largest lexical and other linguistic input from a single West African language or language cluster to have been found in Afro-European Creole languages of the Caribbean.

As indicated by Robertson (1986) and Smith, Robertson and Williamson (1987), among others, at least one third of the core lexical input into this Creole language comes from Eastern Ijo dialects of the Niger Delta area. The words for basic functions like sleep, walk, run and drink, as well as those for body parts are readily derived from Eastern Ijo. *Mingi*, the Eastern Ijo word for "water", may be seen as being among the more significant of these lexical borrowings.

The significance of *mingi* derives from at least two sources. Under any circumstances, the word for "water" would be among the most significant, simply because of the fundamental role that water plays in the maintenance of life. The Berbice Dutch Creole language's use of a word from Eastern Ijo rather than Dutch, the relevant European language in this case, is indicative of the level of significance of the Ijo influence in the colony. This kind of lexical argumentation has already been documented (Smith, Robertson and Williamson 1987).

The word *mingi* takes on even greater significance when the geographic environment from which the Ijos came and that of the Berbice colony to which they were transferred are taken into consideration. The Eastern Ijos are a Niger Delta people, and water is the dominant element in their world. The riverine communities are often overhung with mangrove. The areas around the Berbice and Canje rivers in Guyana have been described by at least one Ijo speaker (a colleague, Otelamate Harry) as being "just like back home" because the Berbice River and its major tributaries, the Canje and the Wieruni, are both overhung with mangrove. It should therefore come as little surprise that at least one significant cultural transfer to the Berbice colony is linked to Ijo religious practices and belief systems that are associated with water:

> Veneration of the ancestors plays a central role in Ijo traditional religion, while water spirits, known as Owuamapu, figure prominently in the Ijaw pantheon. In addition, the Ijaw practice a form of divination called Igbadai, in which recently deceased individuals are interrogated on the causes of their death.
>
> Ijaw religious beliefs hold that water spirits are like humans in having personal strengths and shortcomings, and that human beings dwell among the water spirits before being born. (Alagoa 1964, 7)

According to Horton (n.d.) and Alagoa (1964), it is believed that the spirit returns to some place beneath water after death. From here the ancestors sometimes visit during special celebrations. When they do so, they bring with them the special ability to identify evildoers and those who are working against the general good of the remainder of the slaves. They may also determine appropriate forms of punishment for such persons. The ancestors exercise considerable power through the mediums they inherit when they return.

In the Berbice colony, the worship of Mingi Mamma, literally "Water Mamma", may be linked directly to the Eastern Ijo belief systems. The practice of Mingi Mamma worship and celebration was significant enough to have become the source of considerable concern to the Europeans in the colony. There are perhaps three separate testimonies to the level of significance attached to the practice by the various groups inhabiting the colony at the time.

The first comes from a group that would have consisted of slaves and their descendants on the river. These would have been African in the main but also would have included persons of mixed indigenous Indian and African ancestry. In some instances, the relationships between and among members of these two groups were far from the hostile stereotype often indicated by historians. Often, they were quite intimate.

There is considerable evidence that the practice of Mingi Mamma worship was very prevalent among persons of African descent. The most significant piece of evidence was the "Proclamation of the Governor and Court of Policy against the Practice of Obeah" of 2 April 1810. According to Thompson (2002a, 149), the proclamation read as follows:

> Whereas we have taken into consideration that the Profession of Obiah so generally practiced among the Negroes, or other slaves, is productive of the most calamitous consequences, And in order to suppress[s] that evil, we have thought proper to order and enjoin as follows:
>
> That any negro or other slave who after the publication of these presents, be found guilty of practicing Obiah or pretending to exercise any secret arts, or to possess any . . . supernatural powers, whereby the life, health, or happiness[s], of any other slave or individual may be endangered, such negro or other slave so convicted before this Court, shall suffer Death or such other punishment as the exigency [*sic*] of the case shall appear to require.

The proclamation does not specifically say "Mingi Mamma practice", but uses the general classification of obeah.

In 1819, a proclamation of the Court of Criminal Justice concerning a prisoner named Hans states, as quoted in Thompson (2002a, 149):

> Whereas the Negro Hans of the Congo nation belonging to the Winkel department Prisoner at the Bar, stands accused before his Honor the Fiscal R.O. For that he the prisoner Hans did on the night of the twelfth of June last go to Plantation Demtichem on the East bank of the River Berbice provided with an obiah image and other spells thereunto appertaining, for the purpose of discovering poison, or to remove certain bad things from that estate. Further that he the said Prisoner Hans is in the habit of carrying on a regular Obiah trade, and that he

has exercised his art on different occasions on several Estates within this colony assuming unto himself the possession of supernatural power derived from God.

The prisoner is tried and found guilty. The classification of the practice as "Obiah" is not surprising and may in part be attributed to the ignorance of the Europeans about some of the differences between obeah and Mingi Mamma such that "Obiah" came to be the general name for both practices. In the accompanying documents to the case, however, there is consistent reference to Mingi Mamma.

By contrast, this 1823 proclamation against an accused prisoner named Willem makes specific mention of Mingi Mamma, and the similarities between the two cases suggest that the practice of Mingi Mamma was, in fact, what Hans had been involved in. One section of the proclamation against Willem read,

> Whereas the Negro Willem, alias Sara, alias Cuffey, a Creole, a native of this colony, belonging to Plantation Buses Lust, situated on the east bank of the river Berbice, prisoner, here stands accused by his Honour the Fiscal R.O. of treasonable practices, by deluding the minds of the negroes belonging to plantation Op Hoop van Beter, also situate in this colony, from their obedience to the law of the land, and their proprietors, by dancing or causing to be danced, on the said estate Op Hoop van Beter, the Minje or Water Mamma dance, thereby conspiring with drivers of said estate, and by the severe punishment inflicted by his direction, during the said dance, on the Negroes Madelon, a slave on said estate, thereby causing her death. (as quoted in Thompson 2002a, 149)

This time the reference to Mingi Mamma is clear.

There are several significant issues here. The first is that the practices appeared to have been widespread, at least along the banks of the river. Of even greater significance is the fact that the practices continued even though the proclamation indicated that the punishment would be severe, as indeed it was in the two cases cited here. Willem was to be put to death and his head hung on a pole, both so that all slaves could see and so that he could not fly back to Africa. And Hans had to wear a permanent "halter and the Obiah Image and other spells thereunto appertaining, and used by him the said Prisoner at the Bar, in the exercise of the pretended supernatural power be fastened around his neck, to be severely flogged with rods under the Gallows and then and there to be brand-marked" (Thompson 2002a, 150).

As mentioned, the practices seem to have continued long after a proclamation with draconian punishments had been established to stamp them out had been passed. That they continued is testimony to their significance for the persons who used them – no person would continue an insignificant practice in the face of such severe deterrents. In addition, the practice is known to have been retained into the twentieth century, and even today, some persons are said to be or to have been "Water People".

Even more significant was the fact that the diviners/mediators exerted considerable influence. In the cases of both Hans and Willem, they commanded considerable respect from the black drivers who summoned them to the estates and who participated in the cover-up when Madelon died at the hands of Willem and his followers. They also arranged for the body to be dispensed with.

These two outstanding cases make a very powerful statement about the level of African religious survivals and practices in the Berbice (and perhaps the New World) plantations. Thompson (2002a, 19) describes both Willem and Hans as exorcists and noted that they "exercised considerable influence within slave communities. . . . Both of them were summoned to the estates to discern and eliminate the evil that was causing a rash of sudden deaths there." Thompson noted further that, "whether real or pretended, several persons involved in this dance became completely transformed beings, acting in ways sometimes quite out of character. Hans generated a considerable amount of fear and respect for himself and for his role as a mediator between the human and the spirit worlds. The impact he had on the black population was so evident to the whites that they remarked on it" (19). As for Willem, he showed no sign of concern even after the death of the lady Madelon nor indeed even as he approached his execution, having indicated that he had the power to return to Africa and having also asserted that the whites could not really harm him. According to Thompson (2002a, 19), "he demanded allegiance of the people on the estate even above the allegiance he showed to the white personnel there". And it was Willem's claim to have the power to return to Africa that, simply because of the difference in world view between the Europeans and the Africans, caused his sentence to include the macabre requirement that he be beheaded and his head kept on a pole to show others that he would not – in fact, could not – return to Africa.

In addition, Willem described himself as "Abadi Tobbekie". *Abadi* is the Eastern Ijo word for "ocean" and the Berbice Dutch word for "God". Willem was seeing himself as God's son. The use of the Eastern Ijo word for the ocean to represent God in Berbice Dutch is perhaps a way of underlining the significance of the Water Gods among the Ijos in Berbice. The link of the Berbice Dutch practice to the Ijo practice seems readily justified in the context of New World slavery.

The second testimony to the level of significance of the practice of Mingi Mamma may be linked to the existence of a location 103 miles up the Canje Creek that bears the name "Mingi Mamma". A *yarouilla* tree was planted at the Mingi Mamma location and is still used to mark the area on the Canje Creek. It is one of very few places in the colony that bears an obvious African-derived name and, in this case, an Ijo name. The explanation given by persons living in that area for the use of the African name is itself instructive. Several versions of the story have been collected in the course of field research, but the essential details do not vary much from story to story.

The basic story is one in which children or a child (the number varies from account to account) is playing on the bank of the creek. The child disappears and an Amerindian *piaiman* is summoned to the scene to help to find the child. (Allsopp [1996, 434] defines the Amerindian term *peaiman* (*piaiman, piaye*) as "a medicine man who relieves or removes sickness, evil, or fear (esp of the KANAIMA) in members of his tribal community by ritual methods". The *piaiman* arrives and, using his particular practice, manages to identify the spot at which the child was to be found. He orders the persons to dig and the child is found in the company of the Mingi Mamma, who had already broken the neck of the child. In one version of the story collected in the field, the Amerindian is actually the parent of the child.

The inclusion of the Amerindian is readily explained by the fact that some of these indigenous peoples were workers on plantations and others frequented the plantations to provide those supplies that could not be provided in sufficient quantity by the slaves on the plantations. These Amerindians inhabited the same watery environment as did the slaves and the Ijos in West Africa. They, too, had concern for and worshipped the water spirits. Indeed, it is of interest that the first navigable tributary on the western bank of the Berbice River bears the name "Wieruni". *Uni* is the word for "water" in Lokono, and *hiaru* is the word for "woman". The name "Wieruni" may therefore be analysed as being a combination of "woman" and "water".

There is a parallel story told about a lake called the Mermaid's Lake, located at De Velde on the Berbice River. The dramatic story, told by the Rev. Charles Dance, a missionary in the colony, deserves to be quoted in full (Dance 1881, 42):

> There was a captain of Indians who was also a Piai priest and doctor. He lived on this Savannah. His little daughter went down to the river every day to bathe, and was frequently seen splashing, diving, and swimming with a companion of apparently her own age. Much notice was not taken of her doings, for she was a spoilt and wayward child, and allowed by her fond father to do, and to go whatever or wherever she liked. But one day she was missing. Evening came and the Captain's daughter was not at home. Search was made for her in the river, but without success. At night the piaiman was heard supplicating the spirits of the river and savanna to inspire him with the knowledge of his daughter's fate. At the dawn of day he went down to the river and searched about the bank, rattling his goubi-shak-shak, or magic gourd, as it is indiscriminately called (but properly, as by themselves, eumaracca) and chanting in plaintive and sorrowful tones. At times he would place his ears close to the ground and shake his eumaracca, and listen as if seeking to discover by sound a hollow space under ground – a passage from the river. Thus he went on, forming for himself an irregular path upward to the savanna, until he came to the lake. Here he sat down and in sweetest tones implored for the restitution of his child. There was a motion in the water, and then appeared a mintje mamma, mermaid, or merman, (Guiana legends tend to the belief of the hermaphrodite nature of these mysterious and fabulous creatures) who laughed derisively and tauntingly while swimming about and lashing the water with his tail. Arrow after arrow, with unerring aim, sped from the captain's bow. The merman's head and breast were covered with them. He sank down into the lake. But his descent was for a moment only. He returned, and with him the captain's daughter swimming around and plucking out the

arrows from the head and breast of her mysterious lover. The captain, tantalized and enraged beyond forbearance at this explicit sign of his daughter's unnatural affection, plunged into the pond with his uplifted cutlass, slashing right and left. A terrible commotion ensued. The water everywhere bubbled and foamed. But the captain has never been seen from that day.

The parallels between this story and the story of the Mingi Mamma location are striking. At the core of the story of the Mermaid's Lake is the issue of a child being abducted by some water being. The child is abducted while playing in or near the edge of the river. The being that seizes the child is an inhabitant of the deep river. There is some attempt to use sound to find where the child might be hidden. In all instances, the child is recovered after the intervention of some person with special powers, most of the time an Amerindian. The fact that the Amerindian story uses the term *mintje mamma* to describe the water-dwelling abductor is of great significance. Here, the actual Eastern Ijo term is being attached to a story that is told about an Amerindian captain, and the story is adjusted to include arrows and an actual river creature, a water dog. Although there is no specific identification of the abductor in the stories of the Mingi Mamma location, the assumption is that a mermaid, or "Water Mamma", was the guilty party.

The existence of a parallel story among the Amerindians is not surprising because the similarity in the aquatic environment could easily lead to independent parallel development of the lore. Dance (1881, 43) comments on the relationship between the African descendants on the river and the Amerindians:

> The truth of the adage that "a prophet has no honour in his own country" is exemplified in the mutual faith of Indians in Negro Obeah, and of Negroes in Indian Piaism. When blacks and their descendants of all colours (who may be faithful to the traditions of Obeahism) seek – without obtaining – the expected aid, they resort to the Indian and so the Indian, failing to get the required relief from the *doctors* of his tribe, applies to the black bush doctor. (emphasis added)

In such a cultural context, cultural transfer and even syncretism were highly likely to have taken place. This would give a ready explanation for the similarities noted in this chapter.

However, the use of the Ijo term *mintje mamma* for the abductor in the Amerindian story suggests that the Ijo transfer could be seen as the base for both stories as they were recently recorded, though it is quite possible that they could have developed separately. If this is true the explanation gives further strength to the claim of a fundamental Ijo presence in Berbice.

References

Alagoa, Ebiegberi J. 1964. *The Small Brave City State: A History of Nembe-Brass in the Niget Delta*. Ibadan and Madison: Ibadan University Press and University of Wisconsin Press.

Allsopp, R. 1996. *Dictionary of Caribbean English Usage with a French and Spanish Supplement by Jeannette Allsopp*. Oxford: Oxford University Press.

Dance, Rev. Charles. 1881. *Chapters from a Guianese Log Book*. Georgetown, Demerara: Royal Gazette Establishment.

Horton, Robin. N.d. "The Gods as Guests: An Aspect of Kalabari Religious Life". *Nigeria Magazine*.

Jones, Adam. 1988. *De la Traite à l'Esclavage: Actes du Colloque International sur la Traite des Noirs, Nantes 1985*. Vol. 1. Nantes: Centre de Recherche sur l'Histoire du Monde Atlantique.

Robertson, Ian. 1986. "The Ijo Element in Berbice Dutch and the Pidginisation/Creolisation process". In *Africanisms in Afro-American Language Varieties*, edited by Salikoko Mufwene, 296–316. Athens: University of Georgia Press.

Smith, Norval, Ian Robertson and Kay Williamson. 1987. "The Ijo Element in Berbice Dutch". *Language in Society* 16 (1): 49–89.

Thompson, Alvin. 2002a. *A Documentary History of Slavery in Berbice, 1796–1834*. Georgetown: Free Guyana Press.

———. 2002b. *Unprofitable Servants: Crown Slaves in Berbice, Guyana, 1803–1831*. Kingston: University of the West Indies Press.

Chapter 11

COMFA

Kean Gibson

Introduction

In this chapter I will briefly describe the African religion of Comfa, which has been transformed to suit the Guyanese context in that rather than worshipping direct ancestors, the practitioners worship spirits of the different ethnicities who at one time or another populated Guyana. But although different groups of practitioners worship spirits of different ethnicities, there is a communal spirit which bears no relationship to the divided society in which the religion is created and practised.

Comfa

As noted in Gibson (2001, 1), the word *comfa* "is derived from [the] Twi [word] *O'komfo*, meaning priest, diviner, soothsayer". Allsopp (1996, 165), one of the two sources I cited for that derivation, quotes from Christaller (1933) as follows: "The *kọmfo* pretends to be the interpreter and mouthpiece either of the guardian spirit of a nation, town, or family, or of a soothsaying spirit resorted to in sickness or other calamities." The Comfa religion (also known as Spiritualism or Faithism in Guyana), which has a Bantu origin, is centred on the worship of ancestral spirits. In keeping with the traditions the slaves and African indentured labourers brought with them, a few people still worship their direct ancestors in that they believe that their ancestors play an active role in their everyday lives – bringing good blessings if contracts to honour them in a particular manner are kept, but causing deaths in the family and financial and relationship problems if the contracts with them are broken. The practitioners go to the graveyards to "quiet down" the ancestors if problems arise in their lives because it is believed that the ancestors are the source of the problems. The ritual restores the division between the living and the dead.

Ancestral worship transformed from being familial to being communal in that the spirits are not direct descendants of the practitioners but are descendants of the seven ethnic groups who at one time or another occupied Guyana and thus bear no relationship to the participant. Ancestral worship became a celebration of the history and culture of Guyana. Even though the working spirit may be African, that spirit is not a direct ancestor. The focus is not on direct descendants, but ethnicity. And because there is no direct relationship, the spirits are perceived as gifts from God. The change partly arose from the desire to access all possible forces for a better future, but it was also for the survival of ancestral worship. The colonials were fearful of this practice, called "obeah", and caused strong legal measures to be imposed against it in 1855. On 1 November 1973, the late Prime Minister Forbes Burnham announced that his government would take steps to repeal that part of the constitution that made it a specific offence to practise obeah as long as it was not practised for capitalist gains. The obeah laws were not repealed because the new constitution of 1966, which came into force when Guyana gained independence, gave freedom of worship to all religions. But Burnham's statements gave elite sanction to the religion so practitioners of obeah and Comfa no longer had to hide and operate underground.

The ethnic identities of the seven ancestral spirits are African, Amerindian, Chinese, Dutch, East Indian, English and Spanish. They are entertained, however, in the order of power in the historical space of Guyana.[1] The hierarchical ranking of the Comfa forces is English, Spanish, Chinese, East Indian, Dutch, African and Amerindian, each with its own stereotyped personalities. The notion of rank according to vital force is the basis of the ranking of the ethnic groups and is not so much in keeping with the colonial hierarchical social order as it is indicative of where wealth and power are perceived to be. The Amerindians have neither economic nor political power in Guyanese society and thus are at the bottom of the scale. They do not have the force to influence the lives of others. This group is preceded by Africans. This not surprising, not only from the perspective of the colonial hierarchical order where East Indians were ranked above Africans; currently Africans do not have political nor economic power since both are dominated by East Indians. The Dutch spirits are specifically the *djukas*, who live in neighbouring Suriname. Their function is similar to that of Africans in being able to dispense evil spirits, but Dutch spirits have a reputation for being more powerful than the Guyanese African spirits. On the opposite side of the spiritual realm of spirits from God are those from Mother Earth. These are the graveyard spirits – the *jumbies* – and are spirits of any nationality. In contrast to the spirits from God, the *jumbies* can make you wealthy very quickly by using any means necessary (the acquisition of wealth under God is arduous and slow), they can make you physically and mentally ill, and they can kill you. Although a person dies from a specific medical cause or an accident, the death may be perceived to be caused by an unknown *jumbie* sent by another human being. Thus the function of the *jumbie* is to restore balance between the living and the dead.

The notion of hierarchical order, and therefore inequality, is central to the religion, but Comfa participants welcome diversity. They do not agonize over it; they do not deny it; they accept, accommodate and praise it. I attended a ceremony where the host, singing songs in a mixture of Kikongo and Creole, welcomed a multitude of identities working towards a common end. The reason for the ceremony was that the host had been ill and the illness was blamed on her enemies. The first song expresses the belief that the host would not be ill for long, thus signalling the defeat of her enemies:

> One day me lati
> Songoro me lati

She welcomed the spirits of those who came to support her. Her healer came:

> Open the door leh me sewell come in
> Ring ding shale

A spirit from the sea came:

> Sali water munun bi waiya

A stranger (fairmaid) came from the black water (the creek):

> Blackie watermamma (four times)
> Oh Blackie watermamma
> A stranger dance a ganda.

An African spirit came:

> Oh me bisimbisimbo (twice)
> MomaKromanty oh wa ye oh

An East Indian spirit came from Calcutta:

> Gracie Graciegyal
> An me now from Calcutta
> Gracie Oh.

An Amerindian spirit came to have a good time:

> Koma mi akipalala
> Me don shalalapalala

Other spirits also came to have a good time:

> Diana Dianadaire
> Diana potina Diana potina
> Diana daire

Another spirit received a special invitation:

> You call me and da me koya ye
> A ye koya ye

Dorothy gave her identity on entering:

> Oh Daratiyewangra

The spirit John came to have dinner:

> Ebiyeebiye
> Me a John Metila
> Fairmaid dinner

However, there was conflict in that the spirit of a snake, a carrier of evil, was coming:

> Kama wakama
> Wakamawisibeniwa

The spirit of an old witch came:

> Mama Yetika, koya ye
> Kongomanzola

And a *jumbie* was warned not to enter:

> Jumbie man hey, jumbie you na know me (twice)
> Ask yuhmatijumbie, demsa tell yuh better

The diversity and unity of the gathering was celebrated in a song proclaiming that the cosmopolitan nation was alive and well:

> Yango ma a kore se yango guru
> Awe me a kore se

The spirits were thanked for coming to celebrate with the host:

> Danjedanjefuyu
> Danjedanje me lati
> Danjedanje man a lati

The unity and egalitarianism of the races in the religion contrast with the racially divided society in which the religion is created and practised. It is ironic that participants adhere to a hierarchical order that is oppressive to them – but they subvert it in that participants have English, East Indian and Chinese spirits who work on their behalf, and the participants are thus empowered. There are ceremonies, "Banquets", at which all the ethnic groups are entertained since they all have to work together. I attended a ceremony where the host did the unusual by having a joint entertainment of African and East Indians because in her view the two ethnic groups should work together.

It is also interesting to note that the Bible is the central element of the religion. It is ironic that the element used by the Christian missionaries to suppress African beliefs is at the centre of Comfa. But the Bible provides justification for their beliefs in dreams, visions, fortune telling, spiritual gifts and so on. It provides a cover for their non-Christian beliefs and also provides them with status because people who believe in spirits may be referred to as people who "believe in things". One obeah practitioner told me that "they [nonbelievers] call fortune-telling people 'obeah' but it is alright when in the Bible they are called 'prophets'" (see Gibson 1993, 2001). Thus Comfa is a religion in which participants subjectively attempt to liberate themselves as well as their oppressors.

Comfa shows national representation and makes an attempt to overcome the divisions in society. Practitioners are aware that freedom from oppression lies in cooperation, unity and cultural synthesis. According to Freire (1970, 162), cultural synthesis does not deny the differences between cultural perspectives, but it is based on the differences. Cultural synthesis does not deny the invasion of one cultural perspective by the other, but affirms the undeniable support each gives to the other, rather than seeing one as intrinsically inferior. The oppressed know that it is only by overcoming the contradictions in the society, in the form of unity and national representation, can they be liberated. The creativity and optimism about the future in the realm of liminality turn to fear of the future in the real world and the divisions of the real world remain.

Note

1. *Entertain* is a term practitioners use for their worship of spirits. They entertain them by accepting them, and they worship them at ceremonies.

References

Allsopp, Richard. 1996. *Dictionary of Caribbean English Usage*. Oxford: Oxford University Press.
Christaller, Rev. J.G. 1933. *Dictionary of the Asante and Fante Language Called Tshi (Twi)*. Basel, Switzerland: Basle Evangelical Missionary Society.
Freire, Paulo. 1970. *Pedagogy of the Oppressed*. New York: Continuum.
Gibson, Kean. 1993. *A Celebration of Life: Dances of the African-Guyanese*. Video Documentary. New York: Cinema Guild.
———. 2001. *Comfa Religion and Creole Language in a Caribbean Community*. Albany: State University of New York Press.

Part 5

Caribbean Literature, Music and Dance

Chapter 12

NARRATIVE AS AUTOBIOGRAPHY OF THE FOLK

Velma Pollard

Introduction

I write fiction. Perhaps because I write in the first person most of the time, people sometimes ask me if my writing is autobiographical. And I have been led to wonder how many lives one would have to live to be always writing autobiographies. Then somewhere in print I read the comment that all writing is autobiographical, and I started to rethink my position. Eventually I have come to concede that what I write is autobiography. It is the autobiography of the heroine or hero – a kind of tapestry woven from bits and pieces of several people's biographies. This stream of thinking led me to meditate on narrative and autobiography and brought me to the notion of narrative as autobiography of cities and villages and the people who inhabit them. It is autobiography, not biography, because the villages and people tell their own stories, describe their own lives and expose their own attitudes, though these may be modified by the imagination of the author.

This way of looking links fiction with ethnographic writing. In his introduction to his 1989 work *Drinkers, Drummers, and Decent Folk*, John Stewart, Trinidadian ethnographer and fiction writer, talks about "ethnographically informed literature" and "literary work that is substantially ethnographic" (8). I will introduce in this chapter a review of two texts which may fall within that category and will turn to the analysis of discourse for a framework within which to examine them.

The folk and the environment in which they live and move is the inevitable backdrop against which any main story is told, any main drama is played out, whether it concerns the life of people from among them or from among that other class with which they interact in a subordinate/superordinate relationship.

Foreground/Background

In using the background/foreground opposition in an earlier study (Pollard 1989, 62), I made reference to the distinction in Gestalt psychology between figure and ground in which the figure of any differentiated field stands out from the rest (ground). Other studies of discourse have used other dichotomies: leading part/side parts, main structure/side structure, for example. I have found most comprehensive, however, Wallace's (1982) distinction, a composite of what was articulated in earlier studies and his accompanying explanation: "Included in the foreground, for instance, are the more important events of a narrative, the more important steps of a procedure, the central points of an exposition, the main characters or entities involved in an episode. The background includes events of a lesser importance, subsidiary procedures, secondary points, descriptions, elaborations, digressions and minor characters" (208). I want to relate that description, which applies very easily to the visual and performing arts, to the scribal arts. I will consider the storyline and major characters of any piece of prose fiction as foreground and the setting as background and will examine two stories with that opposition in mind. Background here, however, will not be minor or lesser. Its examination will, in fact, be the focus of this study.

I will look at the villages described in two stories by Olive Senior. One forms the background to the biography of Miss Coolie, the main character in "The Arrival of the Snake Woman", the title story of Senior's second prose collection (Senior 1989). The other is the background to the story of a young girl's reception into two religious communities in "Confirmation Day", from *Summer Lightning*, Senior's (1986) prize-winning collection.

"The Arrival of the Snake Woman" is the story of an East Indian woman's entrance into, and adjustment to, a rural Jamaican village populated almost exclusively by the descendants of enslaved people brought from Africa. Miss Coolie is a member of that community which came indentured from India to the Caribbean in the post-Emancipation period. Miss Coolie's story is told right through to the birth of her children and grandchildren of mixed race. One might judge the time to be early twentieth century.

The focus of this discussion is neither the woman in the first story nor the girl in the second. The concern is the village into which Miss Coolie moves just as it is the environment in which the young girl functions. This is an attempt to construct partial histories and consider some village attitudes. The point of view is not that of the historian looking on from outside. "Auto" has the force of insistence that the villages are themselves revealing their stories. Race, religion and class are the main aspects of village life to be explored here.

Race

The village in which the story "The Arrival of the Snake Woman" is set is Mount Rose, in the Cockpit Country in Jamaica. Mountains surround Mount Rose and serve to cut it off from the outside world and so from most information, including, in this case, the fact that people exist who are neither African like themselves nor European like the parson who preaches in church on Sunday. History books say these people were brought indentured from India to work on estates which slaves had relinquished after emancipation. The local explanation of their presence is different and is put in the mouth of one of the more cosmopolitan villagers, a young man who goes to work in "Bay", the name of any seaport town in Jamaica:

> They bring them all the way cross the sea from a place call India when slavery days end and they come with their man to work the sugar-cane when black people say no, we naa work with the cane no more for them little scrumps a pay. So the government bring in these people fe work in the cane fe nuttn. Dem is the wutlessess set of people, though. Imagine come from so far to tek way black man work. The man dem is a wicked set of beast, man. Don't trifle with them. But the woman them! Whai! (1989, 3)

Of course as the last line suggests, the women are this man's interest. But the description of the historical event is part of the lore that the villagers, who will hardly read books, come to know. And although one may want to suggest that historical fact is what matters, there must be the awareness of the importance of the attitudes of the people, which frequently have nothing to do with fact.

The villagers reject this new and strange creature. She is the Snake Woman because of her sinuous movements under the diaphanous sari. Their attitude to difference in race is not to welcome it, but to be suspicious of it. Minor characters like the neighbours and the fundamentalist parson make uncomplimentary remarks. While Miss Coolie's story and how she conquers the odds around her sit in the foreground, the stories the odds tell or imply, the wrong-headed assumptions which inform attitudes – everything which adds up to the background – are equally instructive and are part of the autobiography which is the concern of this chapter.

Senior allows the "people" to make a distinction between two categories of "white people", the old and the new. Old whites are the remnants of the planter class who had brought the black people to the village as slaves. Over time those people came to look and to behave more and more like black people and as numbers diminished, especially through migration to cities, even came to fear black people. They eventually died off and remain, we may safely guess, only in the faces of their mixed-race descendants.

The new whites, or new arrivals, without the benefit of years of sunshine, looked white. Their arrival caused some consternation because it could be that they had come to reclaim lands occupied by people who would today be described as squatters. Instead of announcing their claim, however, the pale man and his pale wife said, "Let us pray", and they remained long enough to dispel any fear that they might be connected to the old white people even though their facility with words in English made them suspect. The man was Parson Bedlow, who came with his wife intending to evangelize the village into a fundamentalist-style Christianity.

Reverend and Mrs Bedlow also brought barrels of goods sent from America, and they set up a clinic to cure sick people. They could manage "whooping cough, ring worm and running belly, yaws and vomiting sickness, sprain foot and sores" (22). They had strict moral values and forced people to get married at a time when most people were living in faithful concubinage, which they called "sin". Most important for the building of the next generation, the Bedlows were offering book learning in a small schoolhouse they had built.

Religion

The new religion the new white people brought contrasted with the beliefs that had guided the lives of most of the villagers. Their beliefs were represented by Papa Dias, the oldest man in the village (who also had the most land), and by Mother Miracle. Papa was a seer. He was

> a man of *knowledge* and could do *workings* and could divine fate from throwing bisi the way his old Oyo grandfather had taught him, some even said he could summon Shango, god of thunder and do many such things. And his mother's mother was a mulata, the daughter of one of the old masters, and she had passed down to him the white people's eyes and his "puss-eye" in his black skin enabled him to see far and at nights too, people said, even behind him. (15–16) (emphasis in the original)

Mother Miracle was a healer and also a diviner good enough to have found water for a thirsty village in a well she herself dug. She had special skills with which the Reverend Bedlow's people could not compete. She could "take away the effects of grudgefulness and cut-eye, counteract spitefulness, cure love-fever, or the malignancies of guilt which showed itself in mysterious ways could . . . provide relief for a man who had lost his nature or who was tied because a woman had sprinkled something on his food" (22). Her church was happy with the sound of drums and tambourines, compared with Rev. Bedlow's, which was far less loud. A decidedly African component might be observed in the practices associated with both Papa Dias and Mother Miracle, a not unusual phenomenon in a village populated overwhelmingly by the descendants of African people brought to the island as slaves.

The village and how it treats race and religion and its story at a particular time in history are the material that background is made of. Noticeably absent in this story are concerns of class in a society where everybody is poor and presumably of one low class. The ancient white people have already lost their class by the time the chronicle begins.

Class

Let us turn briefly to the background to the next story, one in which class is a significant feature. It is most clearly portrayed in the distinctions between two versions of a Christian ritual. "Confirmation Day" is a far less complex tale than "The Arrival of the Snake Woman". A young girl is being received into the Anglican (Episcopalian) community. She is being "confirmed". Her reverie during the ceremony is concerned not with the present, but with another reception she had undergone earlier, into another and very different church community.

Class distinctions are unmistakeably clear in the background of events and people in the life of the heroine who occupies the foreground of "Confirmation Day". Her grandmother is a shadowy figure "with creamy white hair constantly fuzzing from under her hat" (80). During the ceremony the grandmother weeps as she has done on "other great occasions: the Death of King George and the Coronation" (80). This is the figure of an ageing anglophile, a representative of a dying breed, the Jamaican brown middle class with a deep and abiding reverence for the colonial past. The colour and class remain, but the attitudes have, for the most part, changed.

The established church, in this case the Anglican (Episcopalian), the state religion of Jamaica in earlier times, is represented as part of that picture. The bishop who conducts the confirmation ceremony is portrayed as the village might see him. He "stands there in his robes trimmed with gold chanting words that sound as if he speaks a foreign language" (82). He arrives in a big shiny new car, chauffeur driven. The chauffeur's importance comes from being the bishop's driver, and he looks like the traditional returning migrant worker from Colón, Panama, "with a large watch which he consults ostentatiously" (81), and the village children think that like the Colón man, he cannot read. Note how a figure from the culture, one everybody recognizes in the lines from the folk song on the Colón man takes his place here:

> ask him fi di time an im luk upan di sun . . .
> wid im brass chain a lik im belly
> bam bam bam

The "Other" class is where the heroine's earlier reception into a church community is located. There the pastor is a man of the people, "with no fussy car and driver and watch and chain to pull in and out" (83). The ceremony is baptism by immersion. The pastor takes each person in his arms and dips him or her backwards into the water. The ceremony takes place on the banks of a river.

In the high-status Anglican church, the newly confirmed kneel on a velveteen cushion and the bishop holds a "finely wrought silver cup" in an old church, its plaster peeling away and bats forever "squeaking along with the squeak of the old pipe organ" (84). The church with its predictable order is at one with the house of the shadowy grandmother where mealtimes are fixed. This is in sharp contrast to the home of the mother, who is identified with the church of the riverside baptism. Her house is described as "crazy-mad and disordered".

The class distinctions Senior wishes to underline are made clear in the contrasting ways of becoming a part of communities which worship the same God. Religion is a good choice as a place to locate class divisions because the irony is most clear in such a milieu. All are supposed to be children of the one God, but they do not eat at the same table. They do not meet except in the unusual life story of a young girl. This story is highly focused. It is about religion and class. These aspects of living form the background against which the heroine functions. The reader knows as much about the village, its religious behaviours and its class distinctions as about the young girl who is the central character.

In these two stories, the writer allows villages and the people who inhabit them to narrate their truths as they form the background against which a star individual's tale is told. In both cases, the setting is so rich that it not only supports the main story but also challenges the primacy of the foreground and, indeed, challenges the background/foreground dichotomy which is believed to exist in all stories.

In most of her writing, both poetry and prose, Olive Senior is concerned with a Jamaica which is very complex. She writes about important behaviours as if they were insignificant. The thoughtful reader however, immediately identifies the painful truths the villages speak. In the two stories described here, the narrative gives the autobiography of the locations in which the stories are set.

References

Paul Hopper, ed. 1982. *Typological Studies in Language*. Vol. 1. Amsterdam: John Benjamins.

Pollard, Velma. 1989. "The Particle *en* in Jamaican Creole: A Discourse Related Account". *English World-Wide* 10 (1); 55–68.

Senior, Olive. 1986. *Summer Lightning and Other Stories*. Harlow, UK: Longman.

———. 1989. *The Arrival of the Snake Woman*. Harlow, UK: Longman.

Stewart, John. 1989. *Drinkers, Drummers, and Decent Folk*. New York: State University of New York Press.

Wallace, Stephen. 1982. " Figure and Ground: The Interrelationships of Linguistic Categories". In *Tense and Aspect: Between Semantics and Pragmatics*, edited by Paul Hopper. Amsterdam: John Benjamins Publishing Co.

Chapter 13

THE EFFECTIVE USE OF LITERARY DEVICES IN THE CALYPSO

Claudith Thompson

Introduction

This chapter examines the effective use of literary devices as a major aspect of the style of the lyrics of the calypso. It is the style that ultimately determines the effectiveness of the message because the calypso is a work of art. Sarcasm, irony and humour have been discussed as broad areas, but the emphasis has been on more specific devices, such as personification, pun and metaphor. Calypsos from Guyana, Barbados and Trinidad have been analysed, using the lyrics of Rebel, Tradewinds, Chalkdust, Gabby and Red Plastic Bag.

Defining the Calypso

Music is a form of popular culture and has many different genres. The calypso is a genre that exists throughout the Caribbean. Allsopp (1996, 131) defines the calypso as "a popular satirical song in rhymed verse, now mostly associated with Trinidad, commenting on any recognized figure(s) or aspect(s) of Caribbean social life, and more often performed by a male singer with much body gesture and some extemporization directed at anybody in the audience".

It should be noted that this definition should be expanded to include the other Caribbean countries because they all have calypso competitions. Also, there are many females who have become involved in the singing of calypsos. In its earlier days the calypso was used as a reliable source of news. It was later used for speaking out against political corruption and social ills. Rohlehr (1990a, 2) posits that African music often served the purpose of social control: "The roots of the political calypso in Trinidad lie in the African custom of permitting criticism of one's leaders at specific times, in particular contexts and through the media of song and story."

Allsopp (1996, 16) cites the Efik word *kaisu*, meaning to go on, as a source from which calypso has been derived. Best (2004, 16) cites the West African Hausa term *kaiso*, itself a corruption of *kaito*, an expression of approval and encouragement similar to the word *bravo*. *Kaiso* has taken on the meaning or connotation of a genuine calypso. Rohlehr (2001, 59) blends two theories of the origin of calypso and comes up with an approach that assumes and recognizes that Africans took their "musics" with them wherever they went. These musics supplied a solid core of melodies and rhythms and fulfilled a variety of functions that have not changed.

Characteristics of the Calypso

Best (2004) discusses extemporaneous performance, picong, satire, and call and response as characteristics of the calypso. With reference to extemporaneous performance, he notes that the calypsonian thinks on his feet and composes. Best laments the fact that the contemporary calypso tends to be prepackaged and therefore lacks spontaneity (18). However, some calypsonians when performing live change the words to fit current situations. For example, the Tradewinds in describing cricketers in "Cricket in the Jungle" have substituted Chanderpaul and Lara for Colin Croft and Kallicharran. The calypsonian may also pick on known members of the audience to include them in his lyrics. Again, the Tradewinds, having seen a popular DJ in the audience, sang in "Civilization", "When two days pass and Pancho [a man] ain't bathe he smelling from head to toe."

In the picong there is a trading of words between individuals. In the earlier years in Trinidad, much of this occurred between the Mighty Sparrow and Lord Melody. Sparrow's wife was referred to as Belmont Jackass and Melody's wife was referred to as Madam Dracula.

Satire is usually the main characteristic of the calypso. It is also a major literary device. According to Best (2004): "Satire tends to be associated with biting social and political commentary. It is employed in witty compositions which expose or attack someone or some issue within society" (18). In "Political Lies", the Mighty Rebel accuses the late President Cheddi Jagan of making promises in order to obtain votes, then not fulfilling those promises after being elected.

The use of call and response, in which the chorus responds to the lead singer, has been sustained over the years. The Mighty Rebel makes use of this in the chorus of "Ask the President": "It was lie, lie, lie, the President lie." Red Plastic Bag does the same in "Ragga Ragga" and "Can't Find Me Brother".

Impact of Censorship

It is important to examine censorship of the calypso in order to establish the link between being crude or offensive and being subtle. According to Rohlehr (1990b, 2), censorship influences the way in which a calypsonian presents his message. The calypsonian, being aware of censorship, finds a way of singing in a more subtle way by singing metaphorically. Mighty Chalkdust does this in "Chauffeur Wanted" as he criticizes the new leadership in Trinidad. Red Plastic Bag does this in the lyrics of "The Country Ain't Well", in which he uses the parts of the body to comment on the ills that exist in Barbados (emphasis added):

> The *brain,* centre of control – must be Parliament you see
> The two major parts now split into three, struck by skullduggery
> The *eyes* looking all around – Customs, Coast Guard, Immigration
> Some go past and laugh ha, ha! The country has cataract.

Creighton (2004, 2) comments that censorship of calypsos in Guyana, Trinidad and Barbados generates resistance and controversy. Guyana does not have a formal process of censorship, but the Mashramani Committee is responsible for vetting the lyrics for the calypso competition. Similarly, in Barbados, the National Cultural Foundation has responsibility for the Pic-O-De-Crop tunes, which are the calypsos selected to be in the competition. "Political Lies", by the Mighty Rebel, was not given any airplay after one of the calypso competitions in Guyana. The excuse given was that President Jagan was critically ill, and it would have been inappropriate to play the calypso at that time. After the 2010 competition, Mighty Rebel's calypso "I Know the Man" was not heard again, although he had placed first in the competition.

According to Creighton (2004, 2), devices against censorship produced art forms among enslaved Africans in the Caribbean, who learned to disguise subversive material in artistic production. Sometimes the changing of one line can make a difference. For example, when Sparrow sang "Cuff Them Down", the last line of the chorus, "Then they *love* you eternally" (emphasis added), indicated to some extent the promotion of domestic violence. However, he used a paradox in the last line of the calypso in order to give the opposite impression (emphasis added):

> Black up they eyes and bruise up they knees
> And then they *leave* you eternally

From the foregoing discussion, it is evident that both Rohlehr and Creighton advocate the use of literary devices as a solution to censorship.

Use of Literary Devices

The calypso is really an art form. Therefore it is not just the lyrics that make the calypso effective. The use of literary devices is closely linked to censorship in that when the calypsonian uses similes, metaphors, personification and irony, among other devices, the calypso cannot be said to be smutty or libellous.

Double entendre is used especially in lyrics that have sexual overtones. For example, in "Hit It", Mighty Gabby describes sexual activity as though it is a game of cricket. The imagery of the pasture, the grass, the ball and the bat represents the male and female sexual organs:

> Jill was playing cricket with me on a pasture one day
> She bowling like Sobers and I couldn't get the ball play
> She start with an out swinger that puzzle me
> Every time I make a stroke how I missing she

Humour sometimes forms part of the double entendre. This is quite evident in "Honeymooning Couple", by the Tradewinds. The title itself is suggestive of a sexual encounter. The first two stanzas build up the suspense as both the husband and the wife finally agree to a particular position:

> She seh both awe on top. That's the way it must be
> And the husband seh yes I agree

The climax comes in the following stanza:

> Now I ain't no peep man. Ask anybody
> But two of them on top I got to see.
> So I bend down by the keyhole and put me eye
> And what I saw made me laugh till I cry

At this point the calypsonian seems to be poking fun at the expectant audience waiting for the details of what is taking place. The last stanza makes use of anticlimax so the audience is not treated to the expected sexual details:

> It was a man and he wife and the two a dem on top
> If you see dem in this funny pose
> Well the two a dem sitting down on top a suitcase
> Is a suitcase they trying to close

The Mighty Rebel provides humour in "Second Hand Man". This calypso is an indictment of judges of the calypso competition. He placed second in the competition for six years and this calypso gave him his first crown. His themes are mainly social and political. However, in this song he pokes fun at himself and the judges and is therefore successful in his use of humour:

> I was born the second year in the century
> The second of February
> Two o'clock Monday morning
> Yes my mother keep on explaining
> She seh fuh me you're me second son
> For I throw way the number one
> That's why they should shame
> To give you second again

He also uses the pun to bring out humour in the following stanza (emphasis added):

> The next year I come as President *Hoyte*
> They say I too short; I don't have the *height*
> To portray the boss
> That is why ah loss

The humour is even more evident in the final stanza:

> I mind a girl from the age of three
> Hoping that she will marry to me
> But when a mek me approach to she
> Ah see that she loss she virginity
> So you see I was the second husband fuh she.

Personification

Calypsonians have used personification very effectively. The calypso itself has been personified in lyrics that lament its treatment as an art form. Both Mighty Chalkdust and Red Plastic Bag have written on the deterioration of the calypso using personification. In "Kaiso Sick in the Hospital", Chalkdust laments the present state of the calypso as he compares it with the past. However, he implies that there is hope. He introduces the calypso in his live performance by stating, "The calypso is not dead. It's only sick in the hospital and I happen to be working up there." In this instance, Kaiso is portrayed as a male:

> Once upon a time he walked with his head high in his village and yard
> But up came a gang of outsiders passing by and beat up Kaiso real bad
> The gang ran amok: they cursed in the workplace. Drugs and sex they glorified.
> They called themselves rock, rap, soca, and reggae and Kaiso's house they occupied

In "Kaiso Getting Horn", the calypso is personified as a woman:

> When Shorty took Kaiso to the church
> And gave her in marriage to Mr Soca
> All the guests in the church like Kitch and Scrunter
> Wish them a happy life together
> But soon after the wedding bells over
> Soca start to hook up with all kinds of women

Chalkdust continues with his criticism in the following way:

> But Soca's outside children lack intelligence
> They does dribble and repeat pure nonsense.
> They does walk fast and talk fast like fast food chicken
> And every dress they see they tracking.

By contrast, Red Plastic Bag uses a tone that is not as harsh, but he is just as critical as Chalkdust. His style is to criticize and at the same time show his love for the calypso despite its changing nature. In contrast to Chalkdust, who uses the third person in the two lyrics just cited, Red Plastic Bag uses the second person in "Work of Art", as he addresses the calypso directly:

> Nothing wrong if you fete for a while
> Cause I know that you truly versatile
> But when you get so wicked and wild
> Well I don't like your style.
> But I still love you bad, bad, bad
> I tell you this from my heart
> I still love you bad, bad, bad
> You're truly a work of art.

Personification has also been used in humorous calypsos performed by the Tradewinds. In "Cricket in the Jungle", the animals have all been personified to reflect cricketers at play. This calypso also provides humour as the qualities and attitudes of human beings are demonstrated during the game. From the first stanza, the audience is entertained as the members of the team take up their positions:

> Donkey say me fus I batting; you know I love me cricket
> Crapaud sidong behind the stumps; he say I keeping wicket
> Giraffe and Kangaroo at fine leg; Snake down in the gully
> Umpire Parrot in a tree; he say all right fellas, all you ready?
> Elephant turn and pick up the ball; he say I opening the bowling
> Monkey say boy the size a you; if you say you bowling you bowling.

The climax comes as the Elephant with his dominant strength and power causes confusion with his bowling. He drives fear into the other animals and forces Donkey to abandon the game. This is surely the human condition being presented in the lyrics.

> But Mr. Parrot, the umpire say all you hold some strain
> Elephant that was a no ball; Donkey to bat again
> Donkey turn round and watch parrot; he say parrot shut yuh mout
> You behind safe up inside the tree; no ball me tings, I out.
> All you talking bout hit the man but all you backside inside the stand
> Send some other jackass to bat; this jackass finish with that.

In the final line, the pun on "jackass" is used effectively to highlight the human dilemma. The other name for a donkey is jackass. Also, only a foolish person would willingly oppose one who is more powerful.

Sarcasm and Irony

Almost all of the calypsos sung by Red Plastic Bag (RPB) are highly critical of the political and social issues in Barbados. However, he has been able to juxtapose his criticisms with his national identity so that he does not have the voice of a disillusioned citizen. His patriotism is very evident throughout his political and social commentaries. He uses the full range of literary devices, although a specific one dominates. Irony pervades his work. Watson (2005, 49) states, "As language and words are his strength, Bag relies heavily on his linguistic prowess to deliver his message." Watson cites an investigation into modern Barbadian calypso by Clyde Cadogan (1986, 59), who compares Gabby with RPB and notes that Gabby prefers the "undisguised statement" as his main weapon, whereas RPB uses all the possibilities of the language, including irony, sarcasm, pun and allusion.

Throughout the lyrics of "Not Guilty" there is irony as RPB accuses the government and its functionaries of being responsible for some of the social and economic problems of the society. The title itself is ironic. Here RPB appoints himself as lawyer representing the accused and reads out the charges. He then uses irony to show how guilty they are of wrongdoing:

> They wounded local entertainment
> By only charging twenty per cent
> Petty larceny is big joke for me
> When they move they does move heavy
> They killed no lady with an axe
> Weapon used in this case was tax
> And the aids they have is from foreign money
> Not the one caused by buggery
> Not guilty from the evidence you can see . . .

His winning song in 2009, **"Home Drum"**, examines some of the social ills in Barbados by using sarcasm. Comparisons have been made with global events that have attracted criticisms. However, RPB emphasizes the point that Barbadians need to focus on the problems that exist at home:

> You know how I love my country
> In nationalism I am immersed
> So no matter what issues confront me
> Home drum got to beat first
> Before I sing that while West Indians had 20/20 vision

> They couldn't see de authorities had Stanford under suspicion
> How can I sing bout de fall and bailout of entities on Wall Street
> While their CEO's got big bonuses and went on costly retreat
> Before I sing bout our own Clico who too had to get stimulus
> Home drum got to beat first.

Red Plastic Bag uses paradox to bring out his sarcasm as he comments on the declining morality in Barbados even as the country shows economic progress. This is effectively done in the lyrics of "We Must Rebuild":

> While we building up the countryside and the town
> There is something that seems to be breaking down
> We could have the biggest bank and the fanciest highway
> But what if the people getting worse every day

RPB is honest in his criticisms and spares no political figure or other prominent citizen of Barbados, including members of the priesthood. Therefore, in "Bag of Riddles", he uses the pun in his criticism of a priest who he thinks is too involved in the politics of the country and who uses the pulpit for his own political agenda (emphasis added):

> If you are an Anglican this should be an easy one
> Scratch your head and give it a try
> Tell me who or what am I
> Cause I am a priest; who can ban me now
> St Michael *Row* is St Michael *row*
> I don't have to pray on the seat
> Because is politics I does preach

Conclusion

The calypsos that have been discussed represent a small sample of lyrics that employ literary devices to enhance their effectiveness. (Table 13.1 shows a sample of calypsos and the literary devices present.) It is evident that rhyme and rhythm are the basic characteristics of any calypso. However, what makes the message of a calypso effective is the style of delivery. If the calypso is to be presented as a work of art, the use of literary devices is important. Sarcasm and humour are two broad categories of literary devices, but there is a lot of overlapping. Although a calypso may be said to demonstrate mainly irony or mainly personification, other devices, such as metaphor, simile, pun, and onomatopoeia, may occur in specific stanzas to spice up the lyrics.

Table 13.1. A sample of calypsos and the literary devices present

Calypsonian	Title of lyrics	Sarcasm/irony	Humour	Double entendre	Personification	Metaphor	Pun
Mighty Rebel	Second Hand Man	X	X			X	
	Political Lies	X	X				
	Ask the President	X	X			X	X
Tradewinds	Honeymooning Couple		X	X			
	Cricket in the Jungle		X	X		X	
	Civilization	X	X				
Chalkdust	Kaiso Getting Horn	X			X		
	Kaiso Sick in the Hospital	X			X	X	X
	Chauffeur Wanted	X				X	
Mighty Gabby	Hit It		X	X		X	
	Miss Barbados	X	X				X
Red Plastic Bag	Work of Art	X			X		
	Not Guilty	X					
	Home Drum	X					
	Bag of Riddles	X					X
	We Must Rebuild	X		X			
	The Country Ain't Well	X		X	X		

References

Allsopp, Richard. 1996. *Dictionary of Caribbean English Usage.* Oxford: Oxford University Press.

Best, Curwen. 2004. *Culture @ the Cutting Edge: Tracking Caribbean Popular Music.* Kingston: University of the West Indies Press.

Creighton, Al. 2004. "Censorship and the Calypso". StarbroekNews.com, February 1. Retrieved from http://www.landofsixpeoples.com/news401/ns4020116.htm.

Rohlehr, Gordon. 1990a. *Calypso and Society in Pre-Independence Trinidad.* Port of Spain, Trinidad: Gordon Rohlehr.

———. 1990b "Interview on Calypso and Society". Retrieved from http.//www.silvertorch.com/arts/rohlehr_gl.htm.

———. 2001. "Calypso and Caribbean Identity". In *Bucknell Review: Caribbean Cultural Identities*, edited by Glyne Griffith, 55–72. Lewisburg, PA: Bucknell University Press.

Watson, Elizabeth F. 2005. *Mr Ragga Ragga: Red Plastic Bag.* Barbados: Research Riddims Inc.

Chapter 14

CONSTRUCTING FRENCH CREOLE IDENTITY THROUGH LANGUAGE, MUSIC AND DANCE
A Focus on Guadeloupe and Martinique

Hélène Zamor

Introduction

This chapter examines the way in which French Creole identity has been constructed through language, music and dance from the early days to the present. The first section defines the concept of identity. It also discusses identity issues that have been affecting the French islands in the light of sociopolitical and cultural events. The second section deals with the promotion of the French Creole language and musical genres that arose during the 1970s and 1980s. The third section focuses on the history and the revival of indigenous and European-derived dances such as the bèlè, the gwo ka and the mazurka.

Creolization in the Caribbean

The Caribbean region is linguistically and culturally diversified. The process of creolization produced many Creole languages, dialects, musical genres and dances. According to Allen (2002, 52), the term *creolization* was coined by Caribbean linguists during their first international conference in 1959. Creole languages developed out of contacts between Africans, Europeans and other ethnic groups who came to the New World during colonization. Larksen (1999, 1) and Sheller (2003, 152) explain that anthropologists borrowed the term *creolization* from linguists in order to refer to cultural mixing. Creole languages and culture emerged in a new sociocultural environment which was constructed by uprooted Africans, Europeans, Indians and Chinese after a period of adjustment. A modern view of creolization is expressed by the late Edouard Glissant (2004). The poet defines creolization as a "*métissage d'arts, ou de langues qui produit l'inattendu*". The French "*métissage*" refers to the blend of various artistic forms and languages. This kind of mixture produced unexpected cultural patterns.

The concept of identity has received considerable attention from both Caribbean and international scholars. Identity has been defined as a set of common characteristics shared by a group of people. Premdas (1996, 10), who studies Caribbean identity, writes: "Identity as belonging can be acquired through membership in various communities bound by one or more social attributes such as race, language, religion, culture, region, etc." In the Caribbean and other parts of the world, race and ethnicity are often perceived to be crucial in identifying a specific group of people. For example, Indo-Trinidadians are affiliated with Islam and Hindu religions. Language and history are significant elements in identity. And Dominica, Guadeloupe, Haiti, St Martinique and St Lucia share a common denominator: the French Creole language and culture.

Although Caribbean islands share a similar history, their current political status differs according to their former colonial experiences. In the early 1960s, independence movements arose in the anglophone Caribbean. On 19 March 1946, Guadeloupe and Martinique were granted the political status of Départements Français d'Outre-Mer (French Overseas Departments).

This new political status has since allowed Guadeloupians and Martiniquans to enjoy the same educational and health systems, social benefits, and civil and sociopolitical rights as their Metropolitan French counterparts. This status, that of being a French Caribbean as well as a French citizen, is what has led to the unfortunate split in French Caribbean identity.

After departmentalization, the sociopolitical environment in Guadeloupe and Martinique was unstable. In Schepnel and Prudent's view (1993, 102), there were tensions between the Extremist Party members and the black nationalists belonging to the Parti Progressiste Martiniquais (Martiniquan Progressive Party), whose leader was the late Aimé Césaire, the founder of the Négritude movement in the early 1920s. Black French Caribbean identity was highlighted by Césaire and colleagues Léopold Sedar Senghor and Léon Gontran-Damas in the first half of the twentieth century while they were students in France. The three promoted black culture and writing through the Négritude movement. It was at that time that Césaire wrote the pivotal work coming out of the movement, *Cahier du Retour au Pays Natal* (Notebook of the Return to My Native Land).

For the Extremists, departmentalization was a new form of French colonialism. Martiniquan Creole whites, known as békés, considered it to be a major threat to their economic power and financial interests. In Guadeloupe, leaders of various independence movements were imprisoned after an outbreak of riots throughout the island.

It was in this hostile political environment that identity became a challenge for French Caribbean people. The leaders of the proindependence movements opted for French Creole instead of French as a means of expressing their concerns and opinions. For them, French was the language of the colonial power. The political status and sociolinguistic situation of Guadeloupe and Martinique may have been held responsible for causing identity issues in these territories. Apart from Haiti, French Creole has never gained any official status in the French Caribbean *départements*. French has been the dominant language since colonization, commonly used in formal settings, whereas French Creole is the variety spoken at home, in the streets, and among friends and family members. For a long time, French Creole was associated with vulgarity, lack of education and slavery. Children were frequently scolded and beaten for speaking it in public.

In 1981, Glissant, one of Césaire's adherents, continued to address the problem of identity in his book *Le Discours Antillais* (Caribbean Discourse). He speaks about the "*malaise antillais*" (French West Indian unease). In Glissant's opinion, Martiniquans have been longing for a true identity. He even uses the terms *retour* (return) and *détour* (detour) to describe the personality of his fellow Martiniquans. *Retour* indicates that some Martiniquans strongly cling to their African roots, whereas *détour* refers to a complete rejection of Africa and complete embracement of the European culture.

Dash (2010), who comments on Glissant's view of the writers on the Martiniquan situation explains as follows: "The experience of centuries of almost unbroken assimilation locks Martinique in an unequal neo-colonial relationship with Metropolitan France and separates it from its archipelagic context within the Caribbean" (5). Glissant senses that Martiniquan culture has lost its way and become a "*colonie de consommation*" (consumption colony).

As we know, language is vital in constructing identity. Through language, people express their joys and sorrows and interact with each other. Guilbault (1993, 32) explains that both Guadeloupian and Martiniquan political parties mentioned earlier were using French Creole for their slogans: *Annou Lévé!* (Let Us Get Up!), *Fò Nou Lité* (We Have to Fight) and *Ou Pa Ni Pou Senjé* (You Do Not Have to Imitate). Moreover, French Creole functions as a lingua franca between the French Creole–speaking islands, including Dominica, Guadeloupe, Haiti, Martinique and St Lucia. It is the language of orality and music. Dash (2005, 6) reports that Glissant highlights the effects of the departmentalization law on French Creole as a language. The vernacular has not "lost its dynamism". Glissant notes that French Creole became a patois of French. To justify his point, he explains that a fisherman used the word "*amson*" instead of the Creole word "*zin*" meaning "hook". "*Amson*" derives from French "*hameçon*".

In spite of the language crisis that was plaguing the islands, a couple of artists made efforts to express themselves in some radio programmes. Guilbault (1993, 33) points out the emergence of French Creole radio programmes at the end of the 1970s. From 1969 to 1970, Guadeloupian jazz guitarist Gérard Locquel used French Creole in the programme *Casimir Létang*. A new French Creole orthography was indeed created by the Groupe d'Etudes et de Recherches en Espace Créolophone (GEREC). Martiniquan linguist Jean Bernabé and his colleagues established the GEREC with the purpose of putting a standardized French Creole orthography in place. Guilbault (1993, 12) reports that many French Creole newspapers and magazines began to be produced. The most popular in Martinique were the magazines *Grif An Tè* and *Antilla Kwéyòl*. But, as Berrian (2002, 40) points out, the linguists have not quite managed to solve all the issues related to standardization of the vernacular, among them the "creation of an orthographical system to transcribe Creole into form and the relation between acrolect and basilect Creoles in connection with the emergence of other interlectal forms".

The identity problem also had an impact on French Caribbean music. The origins of the Biguine, another typically French Caribbean dance, remain a mystery. Léardée and Meunier note that musician Ernest Léardée believed that the Biguine arose in Martinique during the nineteenth century. Rosemain (1986, 79) and Cally (1990, 97) argue that Biguine music emerged in the cabarets and casinos of St Pierre (Martinique) by the mid-nineteenth century. As far as Jallier (2000, 29) is concerned, the Biguine was an altered form of the polka. He also claims that musicians Barrel Coppet and Loulou Boislaville had pointed out three main stages of development of the Biguine as a dance. It first developed as a polka, became a quadrille and finally became the Biguine.

The creolization process generated early forms of the Biguine which were identified by Rosemain (1993, 140), Desroches (2000, 4) and Béroard (1997, 20). There were various types of other local dances, such as the bèlè, which originated during the seventeenth century and which is also fused with the Biguine during the creolization process, into such versions as described in the following paragraph. According to Desroches (2004), the Biguine bèlè was invented by plantation slaves. The style features a bèlè drum, a pair of *ti bwa*, a pair of wooden sticks used to sustain the rhythm in bèlè music, the call-and-response singing style, the soloist's improvisation and a certain nasal voice quality.

Béroard (1997, 3) distinguishes between the *biguine de salon* (Biguine for salon) and the *biguine de bal* (Biguine for parties). The *biguine de salon* was accompanied by the piano, the violin and the cello. Urban Biguine was another musical genre that was brought into fashion. Desroches adds that urban Biguine musicians adopted the piano, trombone, clarinet, bass guitar and *shak shak, a musical instrument consisting of a can filled with pebbles and seeds that can be shaken*. The post-Emancipation period was marked by profound political and social disparities between the whites, the free coloureds and the blacks. Most singers who grew up in this socially divided society sang about political matters, including current events, and sentimental relationships between men and women.

As the bèlè developed in modern times, it evolved into two types of musical genres and dances. The first type, called the bèlè linò, has a square formation and features a bèlè drum, a *lavwa* (singer), a *répondè* (chorus), a *ti bwa* player and eight dancers. It is performed in the northeastern part of Martinique and consists of the following rhythms: bèlè, grand bèlè, bélia and marin bouro. The second type of bèlè appeared in the southeastern region of the island. It is called the bèlè lisid (*bèlè du sud*). Informants Pierre Dru, in 2000, and Jean-Claude Lamorandière, in 2002, noted the absence of the square formation in the bèlè lisid. In terms of instrumentation, the bèlè lisid does not feature any *ti bwa*, but in contrast to the bèlè linò, there are two or three bèlè drummers and a *moun a vwa* (soloist). Another drum, the tanbou gwo kou, is also included in the ensemble.

Urie and Urie (1991, 204) similarly trace the origins of the Guadeloupian gwo ka music and dance to the seventeenth century. Like the bèlè, it took root in plantations. Both researchers state that the gwo ka was initially accompanied by a boula drum (smallest drum of the Rada percussion group), a kathabou (smallest of the congo percussion group), a calabash, a triangle and a singer. Informant Jacqueline Thôle, in 2002, described the musical accompaniment of gwo ka. Gwo ka music features a *chantè* (singer), a boula drum, a makchè drum and dancers. The gwo ka dance consists of seven rhythms, including lèwòz, tumblack, grajé, kaladja, minnde, guiambel and woulé.

From the 1920s to the mid-1970s, the Biguine, as a French Caribbean indigenous musical genre featuring high-pitched drums, a brass section, a piano, guitars, shak shak and maracas, underwent changes. By the mid-1970s, it had waned in popularity because of the strong presence of "foreign" musical styles, including the Dominican cadence-lypso, the Cuban salsa, the Haitian cadence-rampa and the konpa. Popular cadence-lypso bands Bill-O-Men, Exile One and Grammacks toured their neighbouring islands on a regular basis. The most famous konpa bands – Tabou Combo, Skah Shah and Volo Volo, to name a few – visited their French Creole counterparts.

Also in the mid-1970s, French Caribbean musicians created a new style called kadans. According to Guilbault (1993, 85), this type of music was highly influenced by the Haitian konpa and the Dominican cadence-lypso. Bands such as Les Aiglons, La Sélecta, Les Vikings de la Guadeloupe/Martinique, Typical Combo, La Perfecta, Opération 78, Les Léopards, Les Maxels and Super Combo produced kadans music. Kadans songs tended to address issues affecting French Caribbean citizens, issues such as unemployment, isolation, politics, migration and others. Singers continued to sing in French Creole, although French might also be mixed in. In La Sélecta's popular "Pa Ni Travail" (There Is No Work), the first two words are written in French Creole whereas the third word is French. "Nou Pé Ké Oublier" (We Are Not Going to Forget), another song by La Sélecta, consists of both French and French Creole words. The first-person plural *"nou"* derives from French *"nous"*. Immediate future markers *"pé ké"* are purely French Creole. Nevertheless, *"oublier"* is a French loan. In other words, the process of aphesis which consists of deleting the first sound of a word did not take place as is usually the case in French Creole. In 1982, Simon Jurad composed "Mwen Enemen'w Doudou" (I Love You Darling). There were some changes in the French Creole spelling of the words in this title. The first-person singular subject pronoun is spelled m-w-e-n instead of m-o-i-n, as in the past. The verb *"enmen"* has its own nasal vowel: *en*. The object pronoun *"ou"* was abbreviated and replaced by the apostrophe and the letter *w*.

In the late 1970s, another musical style, known as zouk, appeared in the French Caribbean musical arena. While living in France, the Guadeloupian trio Pierre-Edouard Décimus, his brother Georges Décimus and Jacob Desvarieux founded the band called Kassav'. Guilbault (1993, 21) indicates that Pierre-Edouard Décimus was aware that French Caribbean music was rarely heard on international radio stations. For Pierre-Edouard Décimus, there was a strong cultural identity problem for French Caribbean groups: they faced fierce international competition because of the high consumption of foreign (but not Caribbean) musical genres, and it was hard for them to be recognized as French Caribbean people. Guilbault (1993, 22) adds that Pierre-Edouard Décimus had a clear purpose in mind – producing a "sound that could be identified unquestionably with the Antilles".

The name of the band, Kassav', was chosen to conjure up images of the cake made of cassava, or *manniòk*. The juice of the cassava has to be extracted in order to avoid intoxication. According to Guilbault (1993, 22), Pierre-Edouard Décimus also says that the name of the band indicates the type of music played as well the fusion of musical genres from which zouk resulted, namely, a mixture of the indigenous music styles of Biguine, gwo ka and bèlè as well as other types of music, including cadence-lypso, cadence-rampa, konpa, salsa, soukous and funk. In other words the name of the band, Kassav', an indigenous food item, fully reflects the indigenous mixture of music that zouk actually is. In terms of instrumentation, zouk bands feature a brass section, electric guitars, synthesizers, a snare drum, a high-hat, a saxophone and a rhythm box. There are two zouk variants: zouk béton and zouk love. The former is associated with Carnival, the latter with romance and love. Berrian (2002, 40) states that Kassav' composers deal with social harmony, emancipation, cultural consciousness, hope, and respect between men and women. They choose French Creole over French because of its poetic effect, and they specifically use the acrolectal form. (Please see editor's comment on this). Zouk did not stop at Kassav', though. Other groups and singers – Azur, Battery Crémil, Créole, Kwak, Météorz, Tanya St Val, Pascal Vallot, Timothée Hérelle, Zouti and many more – joined the zouk craze during the 1980s and the 1990s.

Prior to discussing the revival of the different indigenous styles mentioned in the introduction, it is important to look at their history to understand French Caribbean culture and identity. For instance, the Guadeloupian quadrille and the Martiniquan haute-taille developed out of the French quadrille. The Guadeloupian quadrille comprises seven figures (dances), whereas the haute-taille comprises five. As far as the instrumentation is concerned, African instruments were added to the French quadrille ensemble. Today, Guadeloupian quadrille bands feature a shak shak, a tanbou dibas, a *komandè* (caller), an accordion, a saxophone, a guitar and a boula drum. In Martinique, the haute-taille is accompanied by an accordion, a shak shak, a *komandè* and a siyak. At first, the violin was the main instrument in the French Caribbean quadrille bands, but it was replaced by the accordion. According to Urie and Urie (1991, 68), both the accordion and the guitar were adopted in the mid-twentieth century.

Domestic slaves were able to absorb their masters' culture and learned how to dance quadrilles, mazurkas and the waltz. Gerstin (2003) mentions that the French quadrille was exported into the colony between the 1780s and the 1820s. Developing out of the English country dances and the *contredanses françaises*, it was adapted by Martiniquan slaves who created their own versions of the dance, both urban and rural, incorporating their own cultural elements into it. In Guadeloupe, the dance comprises seven figures, including l'entrée, the waltz, the Biguine, le pantalon, l'eté, la poule and la pastourelle.

A creolized version of the mazurka, the Creole mazurka (which was also known as "mazouk" and was an offshoot of the Polish dance), manifested both a rural and an urban form. It appeared in Martinique around 1830. The rural form was also called the mazurka bèlè, as it was usually accompanied by a bèlè drum. The mazurka bèlè disappeared and gave way entirely to the urban mazurka, usually accompanied by piano, electric guitar, trombones, drums, a chorus, a singer and saxophones.

French Creole identity and culture has been constructed through the efforts of artists and associations since the 1970s. Aware of the loss of their indigenous music and dance, Guadeloupian and Martiniquan associations have been offering classes in bèlè, gwo ka and mazurka. According to Guilbault (1993, 33), Afro-Guadeloupian drums such as the boula and the makè were adopted by members of the Takouta band. Martiniquans have attached a great importance to their *patrimoine culturel* (cultural heritage). The late singer Ti-Emile Casérus and singer Ti Raoul Grivalliers defended their bèlè to the core. The late singer Eugène Mona created *la musique des mornes* (music of the hills). This musical genre featured a bamboo flute shaped like its European counterpart, the transverse flute. Mona was deeply concerned with the status of the black man as a victim of the colonial history and the Martiniquan divided society. Berrian (2002, 117) refers to "Boi Brilé" (Burnt Wood), which Mona produced in 1976. She explains that the singer was inspired by the blues of Louis Armstrong. In my opinion, the message conveyed by Mona deals with our history as well as the present identity of the black man in divided Martiniquan society:

> E mwen ka tann, é sa listwa kite ba nou (I hear what history gives us)
> "Dans les archives, dans les archives" ("in the archives, in the archives")
> Nou nou sé "Bwa Brilé" (We are "burnt wood")
> Tjè nou pa diféran (Our heart is not different)
> Bondyé fè nou pou sa (God made us for that)
> Y ka ba nou lénon blan (He gave us white names)
> Otis té "Bwa Brilé" (Otis was "burnt wood")
> Armstrong té "Bwa Brilé" (Armstrong was "burnt wood")

Berrian (2002, 118) adds that Mona elevated the social status of the mulatto class living in urban areas. Mulattoes perceive themselves as French. The singer took it upon himself to resurrect Afro-Creole culture, society and identity. The late 1970s saw the emergence of the mizik chouval bwa style. The French Creole phrase *"chouval bwa"* means "wooden horse". Mizik chouval bwa is played by bands which were located in the centre of wooden merry-go-rounds. Furthermore, it is closely connected with the *fête patronale* (patron saint festival) in Martinique. Martiniquan percussionist Dédé St Prix is credited with introducing this type of music. St Prix and his former groups Pakatak and Avan Van promoted the French Creole identity of their island by performing and organizing several workshops in the Caribbean. He also toured France and the United States.

The Creolized forms of the quadrille and the mazurka have been fully reabsorbed into the French Caribbean for the past two decades as the French Caribbean asserts its own identity as separate from that of France. In Guadeloupe, various associations have been teaching quadrilles to adults and children since 1987. A *balakadri* (quadrille party) or *balakòdéon* (accordion party) takes place throughout the year except during the lent season.

I perceive the construction of French Creole identity and culture in Guadeloupe and Martinique to be a complex process for two reasons. First of all, the sociopolitical context of both islands is very complex. Second, the language issues arising from the French Overseas Departments have often played a part in shaping identity. Both islands are diglossic: French has always been the prestigious language, whereas French Creole is a nonstandard variety. This has been a determining factor in how Guadeloupians and Martiniquans view their culture and themselves.

French Creole culture went through stages: creolization, Euro-Creole, Afro-Creole. During the first two stages, the French culture and language were dominant. At some point, there was a shift towards indigenous music and dance. However, with globalization, the French Creole music and dance of Guadeloupe and Martinique has spread to other parts of the world and the Caribbean. Every year, Guadeloupians and Martiniquans participate in the Dominican Creole Festival, which takes place in November. As French Creole native speakers, they join their Creole neighbours, with whom they share a common cultural legacy. There is also a World Quadrille Festival held in Martinique in which both French Caribbean and Metropolitan French people take part, obviously a step in the right direction.

Of paramount importance is the symbiotic relationship existing between music and dance in the building of French Creole culture and identity. A large number of music and dance terms have been generated to name dances, musical instruments and steps in Guadeloupe and Martinique. For instance, the names "bèlè linò" and "bèlè lisid" come from the French *bèlè* (*bel air*) *du nord* and *bèlè du sud*, respectively. In Guadeloupe, the word "gwo ka" was formerly written as "gros-ka", meaning "big ka" (big drum). The French phrase *tambour de basque* became "tanbou dibas" (a drum from the Basque region). Thanks to the valuable work of the French Creole–speaking intellectuals, new spelling has been used in the transcription of songs. A close look at Jean-Marie Ragald's song titled "Ou Que

Tu Sois" (Wherever You Are) allows us to analyse certain sentences in written in contemporary French Creole:

> An té dwèt fè ou konpran sé ou sèl (I should have made you understand)
> Mwen té lé (You are the only one I wanted)
> An té dwèt palé di nou (I should have spoken about us)

I will conclude by saying that the revival of the various indigenous music and dance forms has sustained the French Creole language and has gradually changed people's attitude towards it even though it has still not been given the status of national language. As far as identity is concerned, there are still some issues that remain to be resolved, for example, do the Negropolitains, children of French Caribbean descent born in France, consider themselves French or French Caribbean? Clearly, this is a question that will have to be considered in any ongoing discussion on French Creole and French Caribbean identity.

References

Allen, C. 2002. "Creole: The Problem of Definition". In *Questioning Creole: Creolization Discourses in Caribbean Culture*, edited by V. Sheperd and G. L. Richards. Kingston: Ian Randle.
Béroard, M. 1997. *Petite Histoire de la Musique Antillaise*. n.p.: CRDP des Antilles et de la Guyane.
Berrian, B. 2002. *Awakening Spaces*. Chicago: University of Chicago Press.
Cally, Sully. 1990. *Musiques et Danses Afro-Caraïbes*. n.p.: Cally/Lezin.
Dash, Michael. 2010. "Martinique Is Not a Polynesian Island". July. Retrieved from http://www.romangirwan.info/dash-edouard-glissant.
Desroches, M. 2000. "Musical Tradition in Martinique: Between the Local and the Global". August. Retrieved from http://www.uji.estrans/transj2Desroches.htm.
Dru, M. 2002. Interviewed by the author, March 3.
Frazer, A. 2007. "Caribbean Identity. A Martinique Perspective". November. http://ufdcimages.uflib.uf/edu/CA/00/40/38/0000. 23/07/114, http://www.membres.lycos.fr/apawpawle/ngg/Glissant 2004.pdf.
Gerstin, J. 2003. "Musical Revivals and Social Movement in Contemporary Martinique: Ideology, Identity, Ambivalence". In *The African Diaspora: A Musical Perspective*, edited by I. Monson. New York: Routledge.
Glissant, Edouard. 1981. *Le discours antillais*. Paris: Editions Gallimard.
———. 2004. "La Créolisation du Monde Est Irréversible". *Le Monde* 2 (46). Supplément au Monde n° 18641, vendredi 31 décembre 2004, pp. 26–29.
Guilbault, Jocelyne. 1993. *Zouk: World Music in the West Indies*. Chicago: University of Chicago Press.
Jallier, Maurice, and V. Jallier-Prudent. 2000. *Musiques aux Antilles: Zouk à la Mazouk*. Paris: L'Harmattan.
Lamorandière, Jean-Claude. 2002. Interviewed by the author, March 2.
Meunier and Brigitte Léardée, 1991. *La Biguine de l'Oncle Bens*. Paris: Caraïbéennes.
Larksen, E. 1999. "Tu dimmun kréyol". Retrieved from http://fold.vio/noyearthe/Creoles.html.

Premdas, Ralph. 1996. "Ethnicity and Identity in the Caribbean: Decentering a Myth". Working Paper #234, December. Notre Dame, IN: Helen Kellogg Institute for International Studies. Retrieved from http://kellogg.nd.edu/publications/workingpapers/WPS/234.pdf.
Rosemain, J. 1986. *La Musique dans la Société Antillaise*. Paris: L'Harmattan.
———. 1993. *Jazz et biguine*. Paris: L'Harmattan.
Schnepel, Ellen, and Lambert-Félix Prudent. 1993. "Movement in the Francophone Orbit". In *International Journal of the Sociology of Language*. Berlin: Mouton de Gruyter.
Sheller, M. 2003. *Consuming the Caribbean from Arawacks to Zombies*. London: Routledge.
Thôle, Jacqueline. 2002. Interviewed by the author, December 10.
Urie, Alex, and F. Urie. 1991. *Musiques et Musiciens de la Guadeloupe*. n.p.: Région Guadeloupe.

Part 6

Language Issues in Caribbean Schools

Chapter 15

A FOLKLORIC APPROACH TO LITERACY

Addressing Semantic Confusion in a Bilingual Community

Martha F. Isaac

Introduction

The focus of this chapter is the problem of semantic confusion experienced by young students in a bilingual community. I propose a pedagogy that acknowledges the sociocultural contexts of education in a bilingual community as well as the lexical components which are inherently problematic in that context.

Theoretically this work is informed by Tharp's (1994) concept of ethnogenesis (1994), Gonzalez's (1999) ideas about the interface of cognition, culture and language, and Bakhtin's (1991) notion of "heteroglossia". These writers view language as the carrier of cultural and social traits, and this common theme underscores the premise in this chapter that a lexical item in an indigenous language such as French Creole may carry cultural content and meaning available only to members of that speech community. In addition, a lexical item in a colonial language, such as English, may appear similar in sound or form to that of a lexical item in French Creole and consequently present a semantic challenge to the student. Such phenomena must be considered in curriculum construction, and educational practice in the Caribbean bilingual community to which I refer must attempt in a fundamental way to establish linguistic clarity in schools and in the broader community.

As a consequence of the historical contexts of colonialism and slavery, the Caribbean has a rich legacy of cultural mixes, creating a space more often divisive than integrated. I also suggest, therefore, that colonial residues and indigenous modes must be integrated in order to validate the young Caribbean individual. The discussion will be based on a small collection of problematic lexical items selected by teachers in primary schools in two rural districts.

Background

My interest in this problem, which I refer to as semantic confusion, is a natural outcome of the strongly held notion that sociocultural and sociolinguistic factors must form an inherent part of the individual's education, especially in bilingual contexts. The context for this study is the bilingual island of St Lucia where a French lexicon Creole (Kwéyòl) coexists alongside the official language. Fewer children are entering the system as monolingual speakers of Kwéyòl (Garrett 2003), and therefore the classroom challenges vary depending on the native language of the student, which may be Kwéyòl or an English lexicon variety referred to as St Lucian Vernacular English (Garret 2003). However, Kwéyòl persists as a continuing influence, as the examples of semantic confusion provided by teachers indicate. The extent to which semantic confusion poses a difficult problem for the classroom teacher of early primary schools is as yet unclear. The examples came from teachers of six- and seven-year-olds. That the problem occurred at all and still occurs seems sufficient reason for investigation.

Theoretical Influences

It is a generally held belief that two cultures influence the conceptual and semantic development of bilinguals; consequently, two languages and two cultures inform the cognitive process of individuals in such contexts. According to Gonzales (1999), exactly how those two cultures interact appears to be an ongoing debate. I will not address this issue, as my focus comes from a sociolinguistic perspective. What I consider significant is the multidimensional nature of the speech community of which I have first-hand experience, and which is evoked for me by the writings of Bakhtin (1991, 428):

> At any given time, in any given place, there will be a set of conditions – social, historical, meteorological, physiological – that will ensure that a word uttered in that place and at that time will have a meaning different than it would have under any other conditions; all utterances are heteroglot in that they are functions of a matrix of forces practically impossible to recoup, and therefore impossible to resolve.

This notion of heteroglossia resonates personally and finds meaning in the various codes of expression in Caribbean speech communities, especially those like St Lucia, which are bilingual in nature. Bakhtin also notes (1991, 428), "At any given moment . . . a language is stratified not only into dialects but is stratified also into languages that are socio-ideological; languages belonging to professions, to genres, languages peculiar to particular generations etc. This stratification and diversity of speech will spread wider and penetrate to ever deeper levels so long as a language is alive and still in the process of becoming."

This complex sociolinguistic reality must have meaning for young students through the classroom teaching which they experience. Therein lies the connection to Tharp's (1994) proposal of an ethnogenetic approach to education, which suggests an elucidation of the historical circumstances of the contemporary sociolinguistic reality and consequently an understanding and acceptance of the challenges of the contexts of learning. Gonzalez (1999) adds to contemporary notions of cognition the influence of cultural factors.

Semantic Representation: A Result of Sociocultural Influences

Obviously, semantization or connecting language and the mental world or mapping and relating form to meaning is activated through language (Karmiloff-Smith 1985, in Gonzalez 1999). Gonzalez (29) accepts that cognition accounts for linguistic meanings, but that at the same time the sociocultural environment influences the construction of nonverbal meaning and their mapping into words. Consequently, she proposes "a multidimensional model that encompasses cognitive, cultural and linguistic factors" (33). The model can address, according to Gonzalez, the theoretical problem of how similar and different linguistic structures and sociocultural and symbolic meanings in first and second languages influence bilingual children's cognitive and language development.

Gonzalez explains that given that the process of conceptual and language development involves the construction of meaning, then including sociocultural variables is a priority – we need to conceptualize a model that includes the multidimensional interaction of two languages and two cultures in bilingual children. Gonzalez's insistence on inclusion of the sociocultural variables in her model enhances the investigation of semantic mapping and also reinforces the importance of Tharp's (1994) theory of ethnogenesis. Tharp introduces the term to take into account the historical processes of culture of origin. In his words, it is important "to unpack the cultural variable so that differentiating characteristics can be understood. . . . In this way culture can be organized for its variable influence on individuals" (131). In the St Lucian context, the culture variable must not be ignored in education.

Implications for a Useful Pedagogy

Given the historical and developmental contexts of Caribbean societies, every curriculum process must be organized around engagement with the sociohistorical and sociocultural realities of Caribbean life. The characteristic linguistic diversity of these societies is a fundamental outcome of that reality. There are then, of necessity, multiple voices in every speech community. This notion of a plurality of voices and meaning, especially in a bilingual community, must be at the centre of curriculum theory, curriculum design and classroom practice. We need always to consider the multidimensional nature of the students' environment and to make them sensitive to it while developing a pedagogy that addresses semantic confusion and other problematic linguistic issues. In that way students can problematize their own learning and question, understand and mediate the influences of their culture on their use of the target language, thus engaging in a transformative process which heightens identity consciousness. The selections of problematic lexical items made by teachers also manifest other interesting and important dimensions, such as the need for clarity and comprehension about the issues of linguistic structure and the nature and the structure of the vernacular and that of the official language.

Discussion of Data

The data comprise the responses of eight teachers to a request to provide examples of problematic lexical items (see appendix). The contact person from each of the two schools – a principal in one instance and a senior teacher in another – was given an information sheet with an example, and each satisfied me that the concept was understood. Seven of the teachers responding were between the ages of thirty-five and forty-five, and one was between the ages of twenty-five and thirty-five. All the respondents except the youngest claimed to be speakers of French Creole. The youngest teacher, also the only male, provided the most examples. (See the acknowledgements.)

The data are organized into three categories:

1. Lexical items accompanied by examples of student usage
2. Lexical items anticipated as problematic by the teachers
3. Lexical items in which the representation is compromised by inadequate attention to the phonemic issues involved

There were very few examples of category 1, leading therefore to the conclusion that teachers providing the examples were not really experiencing difficulty with this phenomenon, but this is really the first phase of the project and that aspect of the investigation will be addressed as other schools are included.

The examples in category 2 constitute the largest category. The conclusion here is that teachers were able to cite the possibilities, suggesting that there was awareness and therefore that they anticipated the difficulties. The information came from two educational districts, one in the north and one near the south of the island. In the south of the island teachers acknowledged the multiple challenges of Kwéyòl influence, whereas in the northern area, the teachers asserted that the children no longer enter school as Kwéyòl speakers and earlier challenges were significantly reduced. This difference in perspective is not surprising, as the two schools have distinctly different histories of linguistic behaviour.

The examples in category 3 suggest a further phonological complexity in this problem of semantic confusion.

Table 15.1. Words likely to cause semantic confusion for children at the early elementary school level

English word	French Creole/ Kwéyòl word: meaning	Example to illustrate the problem
Category 1 (examples included)		
leave, live	*liv*: "book"	Q: "Where do you live?" A: "My mother did not buy book for me."
had	*had*: "clothing"	"*Ay-see ni had.*" "My sister has clothes."
cannot	*kanot*: "fishing boat"	"Miss, my father have one."
Category 2 (teacher predictions, no examples included)		
wash	*woche*: "stone"	
go	*go*: "big, large"	
cough	*coff*: "a type of fish"	
lie	*lie*: "garlic"	
let	*lèt*: "milk"	
could	*koud*: "sew"	
wear	*wè*: "see"	
may	*mè*: "but"	
fall	*fòl*: "insane"	
glow	*glo*: "water"	
chair	*tjè*: "heart"	
moon	*moun*: "people"	
bomb	*bom*: "bucket"	
book	*bouk*: "male goat", "crayfish"	
shoe	*shou*: "tanya", "eddoes"	
fan	*fan*: "split"	
cock	*cock*: "penis"	
piece	*pis*: "fleas"	
pear	*pè*: "afraid"	
bear	*bè*: "butter"	
tap	*tap*: "slap"	
pot	*pòt*: "cup"	
bow	*bo*: "kiss"	

Table 15.1. Words likely to cause semantic confusion for children at the early elementary school level (*continued*)

English word	French Creole/ Kwéyòl word: meaning	Example to illustrate the problem
pack	*pak*: "fence"	
four	*fò*: "strong"	
low	*lo*: "share", "portion"	
bag	*bag*: "ring"	
pie	*pye, an pye*: "fig"	
lead	*lèd*: "ugly"	
bet	*bèt*: "foolish"	
bat	*bat*: "beat"	
sick	*sik*: "sugar"	
Category 3 (phonemic problems)		
thumb	*famn*: "woman"	
pull	*poul*: "fowl"	
they	*dé*: "two"	

The English "th" phoneme /θ/ is characteristically realized in St Lucian English Creole as /d/, /t/ or /f/. For example, the word *thumb* appears to be pronounced as /fəm/, where /θ/ becomes /f/; hence the teacher makes the assumption or predicts that this will be confused with Kwéyòl *fanm*. In the case of the English word *they*, the word is realized as *dey*, where /ð/ becomes /d/, so the teacher predicts that *dey* will be confused with *dé*, the Kwéyòl word for "two". In the case of *pull*, the teacher predicts it will be confused with *poul*, pronounced /puul/, the Kwéyòl word for "fowl". This complexity suggests the need for training in phonemic awareness as well as in characteristic features of phonological realizations in Caribbean contexts so that language distinctions, whether they are made by students or teachers, can be clear and unambiguous.

Conclusion

A Folkloric Approach to Education

Cultural experience, or folklore, is commonly expressed by linguistic representations. Words like *kanot* and *bouk* are cultural components of the St Lucian environment; as such, they should unquestionably form part of the cultural education of students, not only as lexical items, but with the ambiguities and nuances which accompany them in a bilingual community where the target language has similar-sounding lexical items with entirely different meanings. In suggesting a folkloric approach to education, I am positing that these lexical items which are expressions of the culture should not be peripheral components, but should be brought into the centre of the educational process. Folklore has different functions in society. Among other things, "it can express concepts within a particular cultural context and environmental setting, it can validate culture by justifying its beliefs, it can serve an educational purpose" (Dundes 1965, in Gonzalez 1999, 4). The educational purpose served by culture and folklore ought to be a necessary component of all curricular efforts. Literacy efforts in such bilingual situations must consistently address the lexical realities of these contexts.

Writing about problems encountered in the translation of the New Testament into Kwéyòl, Frank (2004, 1) observed: "To be meaningful and communicative, a translation must take into consideration mismatches between the source language and the receptor language. The translator must constantly make adjustments for differences in lexical range, for differences in word order, for differences in grammar, for differences in idiomatic and figurative usage, and in terms of what can be assumed and what can be made explicit."

This approach to translation may be extended to education in the community because education in bilingual contexts requires linguistic sensitivities similar to that demanded of the art of translation – critical awareness of the social contexts as well as the expressive forms of the two languages. Both Gonzalez (1999) and Tharp (1994) suggest pedagogical practices that facilitate such an approach.

Tharp draws attention to the following:

- The critical importance of developing competence in the language of instruction
- Contextualizing teaching, curriculum and school in the experience, skills and values of the community
- Utilizing the instructional conversation – the basic form of teaching should be through dialogue between teachers and students

Gonzalez suggests the following:

- Cooperation – working with peers to obtain feedback
- Questioning for clarification – asking for repetition or examples
- Formal practice – attempting to increase exposure to the target language
- Functional practice – using the target language in communicative situations

The writers overlap in emphasizing dialogue, questioning, practice and the importance of mastery of the official language.

Given the change in linguistic behaviour in St Lucia in recent times, where many young persons have little competence in the native language (personal experience while investigating changing attitudes towards Kwéyòl in June 2004), the extent of the prevalence of such instances of semantic confusion is unclear. What is clear, however, is the potential for that confusion unless the sociocultural and sociolinguistic dimensions are integrated into the education system. A folkloric approach to education can be achieved by observing some of the aforementioned pedagogical practices. The practices are by no means new and have been suggested by writers in Caribbean contexts and in contexts of multicultural education (Simmons-McDonald et al. 2004; Ladson-Billings 1994; Au 1993; Gallimore and Tharp 1990); in many instances they are already being practised in the St Lucian education system. The need for open dialogue and student engagement at all levels of the education system cannot be ignored.

Follow-Up

Further investigations will be made in the future with regard to the following:

- Determining whether the items which teachers have predicted to be problematic are indeed problematic in those two schools or in other schools in the districts
- Making additions to the current list by soliciting assistance from other schools in the districts
- Planning with schools a workshop to help improve phonemic sensitivity in Kwéyòl and English in the selected schools

Acknowledgements

I am grateful to the following persons for assistance with this project. For collecting completed data forms: Janice Isaac-Flavien, Albertha Eugene. For providing information at Grande Riviere Senior Primary School, principal Catherine Francis, Sylvina Alexander, Sylvia Jordan, Simmons Jules, Bibiana St Rose, and Clitus Jules; and at Babonneau Infant School, principal Christina Joseph, senior teacher Lucia Emilaire, A. Touissant, Christina Matthew, and J. St Edward.

References

Au, Kathryn. 1993. *Literacy Instruction in Multicultural Settings*. New York: Harcourt Brace Jovanovich.

Bakhtin, Mikhail. 1991. *The Dialogic Imagination*. Edited by Michael Holquist. Translated by Caryl Emmerson and Michael Holquist. Austin: University of Texas Press.

Frank, David. 2004. "Cultural Dimensions of Translation into Creole Languages". Paper presented at the Conference on Bible Studies, University of the West Indies, Cave Hill, 24–25 May 2004.

Gallimore, Ronald, and Roland Tharp. 1990. "Teaching Mind in Society: Teaching, Schooling and Literate Discourse". In *Vygotsky and Education: Instructional Implications and Applications of Sociohistorical Psychology*, edited by Luis Moll, 175–205. New York: Cambridge University Press.

Garrett, Paul. 2003. "An 'English Creole' That Isn't: On the Sociohistorical Origins and Linguistic Classification of the Vernacular English of St. Lucia". In *Contact Englishes of the Eastern Caribbean*, edited by Michael Aceto and Jeffrey Williams, 155–210. Amsterdam: John Benjamins Publishing Company.

Gonzalez, Virginia, ed. 1999. *Language and Cognitive Development in Second Language Learning*. Boston: Allyn and Bacon.

Gonzalez, Virginia, and Diane Schallert. 1999. "An Integrative Analysis of the Cognitive Development of Bilingual and Bicultural Children and Adults". In *Language and Cognitive Development in Second Language Learning: Educational Implications for Children and Adults*, edited by V. Gonzalez, 19–55. Boston: Allyn and Bacon.

Ladson-Billings, Gloria. 1994. *The Dreamkeepers: Successful Teachers of African American Children*. San Francisco: Jossey-Bass.

Moll, Luis. 1990. *Vygotsky and Education: Instructional Implications and Applications of Sociohistorical Psychology*. New York: Cambridge University Press.

Simmons-McDonald, Hazel, Martha Isaac, Sylvia Jack and Patrick Allan McDonald. 2004. *Report on Literacy Survey/Reading Diagnostic Project for St. Vincent and the Grenadines*. Project of the School for Graduate Studies and Research and the Faculty of Humanities and Education, University of the West Indies. Cave Hill, Barbados: University of the West Indies.

Tharp, Roland. 1994. "Research Knowledge and Policy Issues in Cultural Diversity in Education". In *Language and Learning: Educating Linguistically Diverse Students*, edited by Beverly McLeod, 129–67 Albany: State University of New York Press.

Appendix: Information Guide

Semantic Confusion in Elementary School Classrooms in St Lucia

A few years ago a second grade teacher told the story of a child's confusion over the word *cannot* in her classroom. She explained that while she was teaching the English word *cannot*, a child raised her hand to inform the class that her father had one – a *kanot*. The child was referring to the French Creole word for "fishing boat".

There are a number of English lexical items, or English words and terms, which are similar in sound to French Creole words. I am in the process of compiling a list of these as well as documenting the stories of the ways in which the confusion and misunderstanding of the students are manifested, for example, the *kanot* story.

I am asking for your assistance in this, by inviting you to provide a list of such instances that you have heard of or that you have encountered in your classroom experience. Your contribution will be acknowledged in all writing on this matter.

The sheet provided has three columns – column 1 is for the English word, and column 2 is for the French Creole word (use a spelling as close to the sound as you can or refer to a French Creole dictionary). In the third column, write the story of how the student's confusion or misunderstanding was manifested. If you do not have a story, the lexical items alone will suffice.

I am very grateful for your assistance.

Chapter 16

BOYS WILL BE BOYS

Gender and Bilingual Education
in a Creole Language Situation

Karen Carpenter and
Hubert Devonish

Introduction

This chapter seeks to explore and examine an unexpected outcome of a body of research surrounding the Bilingual Education Project (BEP) in Jamaica. This project involved the use, for all educational functions, of English, the traditional language of education, and Jamaican Creole (Jamaican) over the first four years of primary education. The project was an outcome of several decades of academic research and some public pressure for the formal incorporation of Jamaican into the education system. The focus of the project was policy, specifically, establishing that the use of the Jamaican language in education would, at minimum, do no harm and, in fact, yield educational dividends.

Concentrating the research effort on providing arguments for and against the formal use of Jamaican in schools produced certain blind spots. These led to results which, as often happens in research, are unforeseen and unexpected and which, with the benefit of hindsight, should have been anticipated. We will look at some of the trends we should have been expecting in the results, specifically those for gender, that have come out of the Bilingual Education Project and examine some of the policy implications.

Why a Bilingual Education Project in Jamaica?

The Conference on Creole Language Studies held in Jamaica in 1959 was the first of its kind. Perhaps, not surprisingly, the issue of the role of the Jamaican language, Jamaican, made an early appearance. At an open forum held during that conference, the matter was heatedly debated. This is documented in Le Page (1961, 114–28). It is against this background that there emerged a large body of research on this subject which is summarized in Craig (1999). The focus of this work was children of the region who were native speakers of a Creole language lexically related to English. The issue was how it might be possible to create conditions within which such children could develop an effective and consistent command of English, the official language of education.

This body of work was produced in the period of the 1960s during which the major territories of the Commonwealth Caribbean gained political independence from Britain. The prevailing model of English language teaching, that of English as a Mother Tongue (EMT), was perceived as not delivering the goods. It had failed to produce sufficient numbers of students finishing or leaving school with the required skill levels in English. Solutions were sought against the background of a perception that the education systems of these countries were in crisis as a result of a failure to effectively teach English (Craig 1971, 376).

The research was based on particular assumptions. It was assumed that the public would not accept the use of the respective Creole languages in school as languages of formal oral instruction, as a subject of instruction, or as a medium for acquiring and using literacy. In addition, the Creole languages supposedly did not have the level of autonomy in relation to English necessary for its formal use in education, given the existence of a continuum relationship between Creole and English. These factors were presumed to preclude English-lexicon Creoles from being formally used in the school systems of those countries having English as the official language and language of education. The absence of a widely accepted standard writing system for these Creole languages was taken as further evidence against the option of accepting these languages as formal languages of instruction and literacy.

These assumptions forced the pioneering research work on language education in the Creole-speaking Commonwealth Caribbean in the direction of what Craig (1999) refers to as the monoliterate transitional bilingual (MTB) approach. This approach supported the transitional oral use of the children's native language, Creole, using the language of the home as a bridge to the language of the school, English. Creole would not, however, be used in writing. The 2001 Language Education Policy (LEP) of the Ministry of Education, Youth and Culture of Jamaica – subsequently tabled in the Jamaican parliament as official policy – is a public policy document which supports this position.

The LEP document (Ministry of Education, Youth and Culture [MOEYC] 2001) reviewed and benefited from the mass of existing research on the subject. Like the research work on which it is based, the LEP viewed the MTB approach as the only viable option. There was a concession that fully bilingual and biliterate transitional bilingualism was ideal for the Jamaican situation. According to the LEP, however, the reality was that these options were impractical. In addition, the LEP, like the research work on which it is based, assumed that Jamaican society would reject formal written Jamaican Creole. The document also declared that there was no standard writing system for Jamaican.

Working from a radically different set of perspectives, as, for example, represented in Devonish (1986; 2007), the Bilingual Education Project (BEP) proposal challenged such received wisdom. What was the evidence to support the view that the public would resist the implementation of a programme using Jamaican alongside English as a formal medium of instruction, as a subject, and as a medium of acquiring and exercising literacy skills in schools? In addition, the BEP proposal also challenged the notions that Jamaican had neither a standard writing system nor the resources needed in technical, educated discourse. It had a campaigning element to it which becomes understandable once we identify the entity which initiated the BEP.

The BEP proposal for primary schools in Jamaica came from the Jamaican Language Unit (JLU), an entity set up in 2002 within the University of the West Indies at the request of the Joint Select Committee of Parliament on a Charter of Rights to the Jamaican Constitution. The unit had been set up to influence public attitudes on the Jamaican language and to popularize the standard writing system for the language. This was so that parliament could find it practical to enshrine the freedom from discrimination on the grounds of language into the new Charter of Rights that was then before the legislature. The JLU put forward the details of a fully bilingual education project in three primary schools in Jamaica. The project sought to establish that options such as full bilingualism and biliterate transitional bilingualism, identified as ideal but impractical by the LEP, could, in fact, be implemented in an effective and sustainable manner. Once this could be demonstrated to be the case, official language education policy would be free to implement these approaches which it considered as ideal, but impractical.

The Theoretical Background

The major justification presented for the BEP was that it would develop in children a competence in both Jamaican and English, the two languages widely used in Jamaica. The various claims in the literature which justify bilingual approaches to education were employed. One of these was that of the cognitive benefits of bilingual education (Craig 1999; Scribner and Cole 1981). The proposal relied on some of the best-documented bodies of research on bilingual education. This was work based on the seven hundred thousand records of minority students in the United States researched by Thomas and Collier (1997) and later publications, Thomas and Collier (2002) and Collier and Thomas (2004). Thomas and Collier (2002, 53–55) demonstrate that fully bilingual education is a predictor of high levels of academic performance, not just in the languages themselves, but in all subjects across the board. This finding influenced the design of the BEP in Jamaica to be fully bilingual and to studiously avoid features characteristic of transitional programmes.

It is worth noting that the model of full bilingual education adopted for the BEP, involving the equal and continuing use of both languages, has come to be deemed "dual language education" (Torres-Guzman 2002). For purposes of this work, however, we shall retain the term *full bilingual education*, in keeping with the terminology used in the original BEP proposal.

Time and the Project Design

In 2004, the Jamaican Language Unit at the University of the West Indies, Mona, approached the Ministry of Education, Youth and Culture (Education Ministry) to gain permission to implement fully bilingual education in a small number of primary schools by way of the Bilingual Education Project (BEP). It would employ English and Jamaican, equally, as languages of oral instruction and written communication, and as subjects to be taught.

The original design of the BEP required that it be implemented over six years, covering the progress of the project group through the entire primary school cycle, from grades one through six. A BEP cohort of children entering first grade in 2004 would be tracked as they progressed through primary school. This six-year period was in keeping with the main research findings on the subject. These sources indicate that pupils had to have been in fully bilingual education for between five and seven years before the positive impact of bilingual education could begin to be measured. After this time, fully bilingually educated pupils pull ahead of monolingually educated ones, and the gap widens over time (Thomas and Collier 1997). There was found to be a lag factor affecting bilingually educated children resulting from their having to develop literacy and other language skills in two languages. This was because the time for exposure to language skills in each of the two languages is half that which children in monolingual education receive in the one language that is used.

The implementation of the BEP required the sanction of the Education Ministry. It granted permission for a pilot BEP to go ahead in three primary schools. However, the advice and wishes of the ministry were that the project not extend into the final two years of primary education. This was the time when the children would be preparing for their national secondary school placement examination, the Grade Six Achievement Test (GSAT), and the BEP being in place during these years might be interpreted as jeopardizing the futures of the participating children. The BEP project which was approved by the Education Ministry for implementation was modified to cover four years, tracking the progress of the 2004 grade one BEP cohort up through grade four.

The BEP saw itself as addressing the main reservations expressed in the LEP (MOEYC 2001) about formally using Jamaican in education, namely: (1) the lack of a standard writing system for the teaching of Jamaican, otherwise referred to by the Education Ministry as the "home language"; (2) the absence of written teaching materials in Jamaican; and (3) the perceived lack of public support for children being educated in Jamaican. There was also an implied concern. Did the demonstrated advantages of fully bilingual education in countries outside the Caribbean transfer to the peculiar language situation of Jamaica?

Whatever the designers of the BEP stated were the goals of the project, its success or failure would be judged by the ministry and the public based on quite different criteria. Rather than on the purely technical demonstration of "how to", as outlined in the project document, the project would be judged on the actual success of full bilingual education which it sought to provide. There was, however, a problem. The indications coming from the research were that improvements relative to monolingual approaches begin to show between five and seven years of schooling. Therefore, shortening the duration of the project to four years ran the risk of results which showed no benefit to the pupils in the project. In fact, there was a strong chance that they still would be showing a performance deficit relative to those pupils outside the BEP, since the project children would still be in a catch-up phase. Such a result would be seized on by the sceptics as proof that the approach was ineffective, if not damaging to the educational development of the child. We had a choice. We could wait, perhaps forever, until perfect conditions allowed us to run a six-year project. In doing so, we would miss the chance of perhaps ever implementing the BEP. We had no choice but to gamble on going ahead in an imperfect situation.

In 2004, the (then) minister, the Hon. Maxine Henry-Wilson, expressed support for the project in person and gave it her blessing. The official letter from the ministry stated that it was "very pleased to be associated with the work undertaken by the Jamaica Language Unit. We fully endorse your proposal to conduct a pilot project in Bilingual education for primary school enrolled in Grades 1–4 in three institutions" (letter, Ministry of Education, Youth and Culture, 6 May 2004).

More than a year later, the Hon. Henry-Wilson was interviewed by a newspaper reporter who was in the process of collecting information for an article which turned out to be quite sympathetic to the project. The comments which the minister was reported to have made are worthy of note:

> But Henry-Wilson, though acknowledging that while the new education policy speaks to some of the issues discussed by the researchers, was noncommittal on implementing bilingual instruction on a formal scale after Devonish's project wraps up in 2008. . . . "They are doing some fieldwork through the . . . formal education system and we would like to see whether in fact the views expressed are true, that is, whether they will prove that the students would be more productive," said the education minister. . . . "But we must be mindful that English is a global language; Patois isn't," she added. . . . "India has their local dialect, but the country recognises the importance of speaking English. . . . One of the assets we need to optimise is that we do have English as a formal language, it's universal, and we need to ensure that our children are able to mine that advantage." (Martin-Wilkins, *Sunday Observer*, 20 November 2005, 8–9)

The minister's commitment or lack thereof to implementing bilingual instruction more generally was, as she stated, dependent on "whether they prove that the students would be more productive" (Martin-Wilkins, 2005, 8). Her definition of what constituted "more productive" was clear – she had expounded on the glorious advantages afforded globally to speakers of English – it was the children's ability to function in English.

The BEP proposal stressed the potential advantages of the BEP for the children's cognitive development. It also addressed the prospect of improved mastery of content subjects. However, given the role which competence in English plays in the social hierarchy of Jamaica, the effect of the BEP on competence in English was critical, as highlighted by the minister's reported remarks. It was this which would determine support for or opposition to a more general implementation of the bilingual approach.

The criterion by which others would judge the project, irrespective of the special time limitations that had to be accepted for its implementation, is that the BEP would produce an increase in language arts skill levels in English among pupils within the project relative to those in traditional modes of instruction.

For purposes of ensuring the validity in the findings, our research focused on what by the beginning of the fourth year was the only group of students that had had four consecutive years of bilingual instruction. These children began with the BEP in grade one of their primary education and had continued in the project through to grade four. It is the results for this group which shall be presented in the subsequent parts of this chapter.

Not So Great Expectations?

The BEP fitted the description of what Collier and Thomas (2004) call a "one-way enrichment dual language programme", that is, a programme which is fully bilingual in L1 and L2 and in which all of the children have the same L1. This fact is significant and of concern to us because, with reference to enormous body of data collected on such programmes in the United States, Collier and Thomas (2004, 5) note: "In every study conducted, we have consistently found that it takes six to eight years for ELLs [English language learners] to reach grade level in L2, and only one-way or two-way enrichment dual language programs have closed the gap in this length of time. No other program has closed the gap in this length of time." These findings are similar to those made in Thomas and Collier (1997, 36, 53). This was critical for us, given the short duration of the project, four years rather than the preferred six.

Collier and Thomas (2004, 5) examined the limitations of all programmes that were not dual language. None of these had been able to close, in the long term, more than half of the achievement gap with native English speakers. Native speakers of English continued to improve their language competence in their L1 even while English language learners try to catch up with them. L1 speakers of English presented a constantly moving target. English language L2 learners, therefore, could only close the gap by making more than one year of progress in their L2 with every year of schooling. It was this which was achieved by children in the dual language enhancement programmes studied by Collier and Thomas (2004). This fact made them stand out relative to all other programme types, including Transitional Bilingualism and English as a Second Language.

We were optimistic in our own situation. The hoped-for positive results for a four-year-long dual language programme was based on a bit more than blind optimism. In the Jamaican context, the moving target problem did not challenge the dual language BEP in quite the way it might have done elsewhere. In Jamaica, the comparison group were not L1 speakers of English who were being taught monolingually in their L1. Rather, they were the non-BEP children of the same grade within the same primary school. They, like the BEP group, were not native speakers of English and had Jamaican as their L1. This latter group was being taught using hybrid approaches, including that of EMT. They as a target group were not, therefore, moving as quickly as they would have had they been native speakers of English being taught in English. This made the four-year target date seem marginally more achievable than otherwise might have been the case.

The Grade 4 Literacy Test

The Education Ministry, as part of its normal functions, had the Grade 4 Literacy Test, a national test, administered to all fourth grade children. It was taken towards the end of the school year, in the May–June period. The results were used as a guide to the literacy competence of children in grade four. In cases where children failed the test, an Education Ministry–mandated intervention took place to get the children to a point where they could pass the test and move on to grade five.

We were interested in the results of tests administered in the May–June 2008 period, the time at which the BEP pupils and their non-BEP counterparts within the project school would have completed grade four. The test came in two parts. The first, which can be labelled Test 1, was made up of Word Recognition and Reading Comprehension components. Word Recognition consisted of forty questions. In twenty of these, pupils were required to *match the picture with the correct word,* selecting from a list of four words. For the remaining twenty questions, students had to *match the word with the correct picture,* choosing from one of four pictures. The Reading Comprehension component had seven passages and thirty questions in total. Students were required to read the passages carefully before choosing their answers to each question from the possible A, B, C or D.

In Test 2, there were two writing tasks. In Task 1, pupils were asked to complete a registration form to join their local library. Task 2 was a letter-writing activity.

The Research Questions: BEP versus Non-BEP / Boys versus Girls

This section focuses on the scores for the nationally administered Grade 4 Literacy Test for two groups of children at the project school. As already noted, the assignment to a particular one of the three class streams in grade one at the project school was random. The composition of the particular grade one stream which became the BEP group was, therefore, equally random. This group, the BEP group, received four years of instruction in both Jamaican and English, with literacy being taught in both languages. The other group, the non-BEP group, received education in the traditional manner, for the same four-year period, with English officially being the sole/main medium of oral instruction and the only language of literacy.

The data for the nationally administered Grade 4 Literacy Test in English, presented below, divides students' performances into three categories: Mastery, Near Mastery, and Non-Mastery. The Education Ministry uses the categories when publishing their results. The method by which the ministry assigns a mix of scores for a particular pupil (i.e. Mastery, Near Mastery and Non-Mastery) is not explained in the ministry documents and has not been made clear to us. There are three subtests on which the children are examined, Word Recognition, Reading Comprehension and the Communication Task. Here we simply present the data for Overall Results, as these have been presented in the records held by the school for the respective children. We extracted the results for each BEP and non-BEP child and created an amalgamated set of results.

This analysis was aimed at helping us arrive at some understanding of the possible impact of the BEP on the (thirty-four participating children) versus the non-BEP (seventy-seven participating children) with regard to their performance on the Grade 4 Literacy Test. Because the issue of gender is a major talking point in discussions about education performance in Jamaica, we also separated the data in relation to gender and decided to identify what effects gender might have on these results. When broken down by gender the sample distribution was BEP: sixteen girls, seventeen boys and non-BEP: twenty-eight girls, forty-eight boys). The questions we sought to answer, therefore, were:

- What was the impact if any, of the academic programme pursued by pupils, that is, BEP versus non-BEP, on results?
- What was the influence, if any, of gender on results in each of the two groups?
- What was the differential impact of gender, if any, across the two groups?

The Results

We present in table 16.1 the overall mean scores for BEP and non-BEP pupils; for BEP and non-BEP boys, and for BEP and non-BEP girls.

The Analysis

Given the size of the BEP and non-BEP groups, these figures can be used for no more than a discussion of possible trends. The composite results in column 4 form part of the official record of the performance of each individual child and are used for determining which children "failed". There was, interestingly, a trend that

Table 16.1. Grade 4 Literacy Test results

Bilingual Education Programme (33 Students)				
Gender	Word Recognition	Reading Comprehension	Communication Task	Overall Results
Girls (16) 48.48	15 mastery 93.7%	14 mastery 87.5%	13 mastery 81.25%	13 mastery 81.25%
	1 non-mastery 6.3%	2 non-mastery 12.5%	3 non-mastery 18.75%	3 almost mastery 18.75%
Boys (17) 51.51%	15 mastery 88.2%	16 mastery 94.1%	14 mastery 82.4%	14 mastery 82.3%
	2 non-mastery 11.8%	1 non-mastery 5.9%	3 non-mastery 17.6%	1 non-mastery 5.9%
				2 Almost mastery 11.8%
Totals 100%	30 mastery 90.9%	30 mastery 90.9%	27 mastery 81.8%	27 mastery 81.8%
	3 non-mastery 9.09%	3 non-mastery 9.1%	6 non-mastery 18.2%	1 non-mastery 3%
				5 almost mastery 15.2%

suggested that from the perspective of Mastery, the BEP group, at 81.8 per cent, outperforms the non-BEP group, at 77.3 per cent.

Viewed from the perspective of Non-Mastery, we see a similar trend, with 3.3 per cent for the BEP group and 10.52 per cent for the non-BEP group. One interpretation of these trends would be that the BEP seemed to be producing a positive effect on the BEP group performance as compared with the non-BEP group. However, the BEP group had almost the same number of girls as boys, whereas the non-BEP group had nearly twice as many boys as girls. That gender is a relevant factor can be seen by the following national statistics (table 16.2) for the Grade 4 Literacy Test for 2008, the year in which the BEP and non-BEP pupils did that test.

Table 16.2. Grade 4 Literacy Test results

	Non Bilingual Education Programme (75)			
Gender	Word Recognition	Reading Comprehension	Communication Task	Overall Results
Girls (28)	28 mastery 100%	25 mastery 89.3%	27 mastery 96.4%	25 mastery 89.3%
		3 non-mastery 10.7%	1 non-mastery 3.6%	3 non-mastery 10.7%
Boys (47)	42 mastery 89.4%	37 mastery 78.7%	37 mastery 78.7%	33 mastery 70.2%
	5 non-mastery 10.6%	10 non-mastery 21.3%	6 non-mastery 12.8%	6 non-mastery 12.8%
			4 almost mastery 8.5%	8 almost mastery 17%
Totals 100%	70 mastery 93.3%	62 mastery 82.7%	64 mastery 85.4%	58 mastery 77.3%
	5 non-mastery 6.7%	13 non-mastery 17.3%	7 non-mastery 9.3%	9 non-mastery 12%
			4 almost mastery 5.3%	8 almost mastery 10.7%

Given the national trend in 2008 for girls to outperform boys by margins up to 18 per cent (for reading comprehension and writing), we have an alternative explanation for the seemingly better performance of the BEP group. This could have been the result of there being a higher proportion of girls in the BEP group as compared with the non-BEP group.

Against this background, therefore, we need to attempt for our own BEP/non-BEP data a breakdown of the figures along gender lines. Table 16.3 presents the Grade 4 Literacy Test Mastery results, from tables 16.1 and 16.2, in descending order of overall performance (column 4, bolded), for the boys and the girls in each of these two groups.

Now that we have injected gender-based differentiation, a quite different picture emerges. The national norms in which girls outperform boys are maintained for the non-BEP groups. This impression is confirmed by a chi-square test of the contingency between *mastery* (coded as Yes or No) and *gender*. For the non-BEP girls, twenty-five achieved mastery and three did not; and for the non-BEP boys, thirty-three achieved mastery and fifteen did not (Pearson chi-square = 4.13, with 1 degree of freedom, $p < 0.05$). However, within the BEP group, the boys perform at about the same level as the girls, 82.35 per cent versus 81.25 per cent Mastery overall, respectively.

The accepted position, as, for example, expressed by Collier and Thomas (2004, 5), is that children in fully bilingual education programmes lag behind colleagues in monolingual programmes until the end of the sixth year or thereabouts. Our data in table 16.3 are taken from a bilingual education programme which had been running for only four years. The BEP girls behave normally and are demonstrating the lag (compared with non-BEP girls) which the literature would lead us to expect at this stage. The BEP boys, by contrast, potentially represent a special response to the gender-marked language situation in Jamaica. They perform at roughly the same level as their BEP girl counterparts and instead of lagging behind the non-BEP boys, as the literature might lead us to expect at this stage, they are performing better than they are. This latter establishes the fact that the boys' improved performance was not simply a result of the BEP girls performing worse than their non-BEP counterparts.

Table 16.3. Rank order listing mastery results

Non-BEP girls	100%, 89.3%, 96.42%, **89.3%**
BEP boys	88.23%, 94.11%, 82.35%, **82.35%**
BEP girls	93.75%, 87.5%, 81.25%, **81.25%**
Non-BEP boys	93.42%, 81.57%, 84.21%, **76.31%**

What accounts for the trend that suggests a positive effect of BEP only on the boys? An explanation for this can be found in the background linguistic situation in Jamaica.

Supporting Evidence: (1) Gender-Based Language Attitudes and Usage Among Jamaican Children

As far back as Craig (1971), we find some reference to gender-related phenomena among girls and boys in Jamaican primary schools. He notes, with reference to a group of first grade children, that, "in one or two instances, boys, when not aware of being observed by teachers, etc., amused themselves by a somewhat exaggerated mimicry of girlish voices conveying bits of standard speech. The point of the mimicry seemed to be *that femininity or lack of toughness was to be associated with standard speech*" (emphasis in the original) (Craig 1971, 381).

These children were being exposed to six months of what might be described as experimental transitional monoliterate bilingual instruction. The findings were that although there were no significant differences in the production of English forms among boys and girls at the beginning of the programme, "girls' speech changed more extensively towards the prestige norms than boys did" (Craig 1971, 381). The inference is clear. If boys have negative attitudes to English, even with the same exposure to the language as girls they are likely to acquire less competence and/or will be less likely to seek to demonstrate such competence in any interaction situation.

Supporting Evidence: (2) Gender-Based Language Attitudes and Usage Among Jamaican Adults

The 2005 Language Attitude Survey (LAS) was based on a sample of one thousand adult informants across Jamaica, and it was carried out in the year following the start of the BEP. Focusing on the results most relevant to the BEP, when respondents were asked what they thought about Jamaican being made an official language alongside English, the total percentage of those in favour of this proposal was 68.5 per cent. When asked which of two possible schools respondents thought would be best for Jamaican children, 71.1 per cent opted for the school in which children were taught to read and write in Jamaican and English as opposed to one in which only English was used. The conclusion from this, after the fact, was that the BEP-type approach did indeed have majority public support, contrary to the unsubstantiated claim made in the LEP (MOEYC 2001) that the opposite was true.

There were, however, significant differences across genders. In the LAS (2005, 13, 21, 38), the dominant tendency was for men of all groups and types to report (i) more use of Jamaican than women; (ii) less use of English than women; (iii) more positive attitudes to Jamaican than women; and (iv) less positive attitudes to

English than women. These results were consistent with the reported association of the use of English with femininity and Jamaican with masculinity.

Findings

It is worthy of note that a search of the seminal works by Collier and Thomas (2004) and Thomas and Collier (1997; 2002) reveal no reference to gender. Whether the original data they worked with did not segregate the seven hundred thousand records into male and female or they chose to aggregate them is not clear. There was, therefore, nothing in the main body of literature on bilingual/dual language education to suggest that the gender effect would have been one which we should have looked for. Nevertheless, given the facts of the Jamaican language situation, both among adults and among children, the gender-related trends should not have caught us by surprise.

Based on the gender-related cultural attributes associated with English and Jamaican, the introduction of the formal use of Jamaican into the education system via the BEP was bound to have had a disproportionate effect on the boys in the sample as compared with the girls. The use of Jamaican would have been regarded by boys as recognizing and supporting their masculinity. This, in turn, would have produced a buy-in to the education process which would not have affected the BEP girls. At the end of the fourth year, when the Grade 4 Literacy Test was administered, the BEP girls lagged behind the non-BEP groups because they are "normal". They were not getting the extra advantage which the boys received from having a "masculine" language added to the "feminine" one being used in instruction. They were merely suffering from the lag created by less exposure to English when compared with the non-BEP girls. Based on the established patterns for bilingual education programmes, the girls would have to wait for the normal peaking in performance which begins at the end of six years of fully bilingual education.

Policy Implications

The language education issue, and the education issue in general, is increasingly being presented in Jamaica as a crisis affecting boys, and the crisis is increasingly being framed as a literacy issue. Literacy has to be expressed in a language, and the only language of literacy within the Jamaican education system at large is English. Any literacy crisis is, therefore, in large measure, a language crisis also. Inability or unwillingness to use English equates with being unable to demonstrate literacy skills.

On the part of the policy makers within the Education Ministry, there is an increasing willingness to do anything which might integrate low performers, predominantly boys, into the education system. A linguistically conservative education policy structure is being forced to look for innovative solutions to what it sees as its literacy problems. These are most acute among the males within the education system. Do the advocates of good education practice relate to a dual language education focus on making proposals for that section of the school population about which there is most desperation?

The problem with the above is that making recommendations on the basis of the evidence we have presented so far would be premature. There is some statistical significance to be seen, based on the chi-square test, in the superior performances of non-BEP girls and boys. This is in contrast to the figures for the non-BEPs, whose performance is almost identical across the genders. There is, however, the possibility that were the BEP to have been implemented over six rather than four years, the BEP girls may have caught up with the BEP boys.

The way forward is for a new and expanded BEP. A proposal for just this was made in an October 2010 JLU presentation reporting on the BEP to the Senior Policy Group of the Education Ministry, which included the current minister. The JLU proposed that a ministry-resourced BEP involving three to four schools, a larger number of children, and covering the entire six years of primary education be implemented. Larger numbers over the minimum period required to see the full effects of bilingual education would greatly improve the reliability of the results. Policy makers would be in a better position at the end of such a project to develop policy informed by the outcomes.

Sadly, the implementation of the proposed new BEP may be longer in coming than one might have hoped for. The Hon. Andrew Holness, the minister of education, youth and culture at the time of writing and the one who immediately succeeded Henry-Wilson, is quoted in the *Jamaica Observer* as insisting that English must be the "predominant language of the classroom" (Budd 2011). When presented with the argument that the failure to teach the Jamaican language as a subject and use it as a medium of instruction in the classroom would be exclusionary, he is reported as saying, "I don't buy this argument that I am excluding people because they can't speak English . . . We must put this language debate to rest." It is significant that the minister seeks to justify his position via a statement that he did not "buy this argument" (Budd 2011). As reported in the article, the minister fails to address the substance of the proposal being made for bilingual education. It would be ironic if the trends we have observed are maintained with more data and over a longer time period. It would be the boys, about whom the minister has expressed particular concern, who would be most negatively affected by a failure to try bilingual education as a policy option. The struggle for language education policies based on evidence rather than opinion continues.

References

Budd, Janice. 2011. "Holness Emphasizes Importance of Speaking English". *Jamaica Observer*, 12 October 2011. Retrieved from http://m.jamaicaobserver.com/mobile/news/Holness-emphasises-importance-of-speaking-English_9878283.

Collier, V., and W. Thomas. 2004. "The Astounding Effectiveness of Dual Language Education for All". *NABE Journal of Research and Practice* 2 (1): 1–20.

Craig, Dennis. 1971. "Education and Creole English in the West Indies: Some Sociolinguistic Factors". In *Pidginization and Creolization of Languages*, edited by Dell Hymes, 371–92. Cambridge: Cambridge University Press.

———. 1999. *Teaching Language and Literacy: Policies and Procedures for Vernacular Situations*. Georgetown, Guyana: Education and Development Services.

Devonish, Hubert. 1986. *Language and Liberation: Creole Language Politics in the Caribbean*. Kingston: Arawak Publications.

Jamaican Language Unit. 2005. *The National Language Attitude Survey of Jamaica*. Kingston: University of the West Indies. Retrieved from http://www.mona.uwi.edu/dllp/jlu/project.

Le Page, Robert B., ed. 1961. *Creole Language Studies II*. London: Macmillan.

Ministry of Education, Youth and Culture. n.d. "Rubric for Scoring the Communication Task". Retrieved from http://www.moec.gov.jm/divisions/ed/assessment/workshop_presentations/workshop_2_.

———. 2001. "Draft: Language Education Policy". Kingston: Ministry of Education, Youth and Culture. Retrieved from http://www.moec.gov.jm/policies/languagepolicy.pdf.

———. 2004. Letter to the Bilingual Education Project from the Permanent Secretary, 6 May 2004.

Scribner, Sylvia, and Margaret Cole. 1981. *The Psychology of Literacy*. Cambridge, MA: Harvard University Press.

Thomas, W., and Virginia Collier. 1997. *School Effectiveness for Language Minority Students*. Washington, DC: National Clearinghouse for Bilingual Education. Retrieved from http://www.ncbe.gwu.edu/ncbepubs/resources/effectivness/thomas-collier97.pdf.

———. 2002. *A National Study of School Effectiveness for Language Minority Students' Long-Term Academic Achievement*. Berkeley: University of California Center for Research on Education, Diversity and Excellence. Retrieved from the eScholarship Repository, http://repositories.cdlib.org/crede/finalrpts/1_1_final.

Torres-Guzman, María Emilia. 2002. "Dual Language Programs: Key Features and Results". *Directions in Language Education, National Clearinghouse for Bilingual Education*, Spring (14): 1–16.

CONTRIBUTORS

Jeannette Allsopp is Director of the Centre for Caribbean Lexicography and Lecturer in Caribbean lexicography and linguistics, University of the West Indies, Cave Hill, Barbados. Her publications include the *Caribbean Multilingual Dictionary* and contributions to the *Oxford History of English Lexicography* and the *Encyclopedia of the African Diaspora*.

John R. Rickford is J.E. Wallace Sterling Professor of Linguistics and the Humanities, Courtesy Professor in Education, and Pritzker Fellow in Undergraduate Studies, Stanford University, Stanford, California. His publications include *Dimensions of a Creole Continuum; Spoken Soul: The Story of Black English* (co-authored with Russell J. Rickford); *Creole Genesis, Attitudes and Discourse: Studies Celebrating Charlene Sato* (co-edited with Suzanne Romaine); and *Style and Sociolinguistic Variation* (co-edited with Penny Eckert).

Mervyn C. Alleyne is Professor Emeritus, University of the West Indies, Mona, Jamaica, and Professor, Department of English, University of Puerto Rico, Rio Piedras. His publications include *Les Noms des Vents en Gallo Roman*; *Comparative Afro-American*; *Roots of Jamaican Culture*; and *The Construction and Representation of Race and Ethnicity in the Caribbean and the World*.

Karen Carpenter is Research Fellow, Jamaican Language Unit/Unit for Caribbean Language Research, University of the West Indies, Mona, Jamaica.

Pauline Christie, now retired, was Senior Lecturer, Department of Language, Linguistics and Philosophy, University of the West Indies, Mona, Jamaica. Her publications include *Caribbean Language Issues Old and New, Due Respect: Papers on English and English-Related Creoles in the Caribbean* and *Language in Jamaica*.

Hubert Devonish is Professor of Linguistics, University of the West Indies, Mona, Jamaica.

Walter F. Edwards is Professor of Linguistics and Director of the Humanities Center, Wayne State University, Detroit, Michigan. His publications include *Verb Phrase Patterns in Black English and Creole* (co-edited with Donald Winford).

Kean Gibson is Professor of Linguistics and Anthropology, University of the West Indies, Cave Hill, Barbados. Her publications include *Comfa Religion and*

Creole Language in a Caribbean Community; *The Cycle of Racial Oppression in Guyana*; and *Sacred Duty: Hinduism and Violence in Guyana*.

Alim Hosein is Lecturer in Linguistics, Department of Language and Cultural Studies, University of Guyana.

Martha F. Isaac, now retired, was Lecturer in Sociolinguistics, University of the West Indies, Cave Hill, Barbados.

Velma Pollard, now retired, was Senior Lecturer in Language Education, University of the West Indies, Mona, Jamaica. Her publications include *From Jamaican Creole to Standard English: A Handbook for Teachers*, *Dread Talk: The Language of Rastafari*, and the novella *Karl* and several other works of creative writing.

Ian E. Robertson is Academic Director of the Evening University and retired Professor of Linguistics, University of the West Indies, St Augustine, Trinidad and Tobago. His publications include *Exploring the Boundaries of Caribbean Creole Languages* (co-edited with Hazel Simmons McDonald).

Hazel Simmons-McDonald is Professor of Applied Linguistics, University of the West Indies Cave Hill, Barbados, and Pro Vice Chancellor and Principal, Open Campus, University of the West Indies. Her publications *Exploring the Boundaries of Caribbean Creole Languages* (co-edited with Ian Robertson).

John Simpson is a Fellow of Kellogg College, Oxford, and chief editor of the *Oxford English Dictionary*. His other publications include the *Concise Oxford Dictionary of Proverbs* and the *Oxford Dictionary of Modern Slang* (co-edited with John Ayto).

Claudith Thompson is Lecturer in Literacy Studies, School of Education and Humanities, University of Guyana.

Lise Winer is Professor and Graduate Program Director, Department of Integrated Studies in Education, McGill University, Montreal, Canada. Her publications include *Badjohns, Bhaaji and Banknote Blue: Essays on the Social History of Language in Trinidad & Tobago* and the *Dictionary of the English/Creole of Trinidad & Tobago*.

Hélène Zamor is Lecturer in French Language, University of the West Indies, Cave Hill, Barbados.

www.ingramcontent.com/pod-product-compliance
Lightning Source LLC
Chambersburg PA
CBHW021830300426
44114CB00009BA/390